CAMPAIGN 346

YALU 1950–51

The Chinese spring the trap on MacArthur

CLAYTON K.S. CHUN ILLUSTRATED BY JOHNNY SHUMATE
Series editor Marcus Cowper

OSPREY PUBLISHING
Bloomsbury Publishing Plc
PO Box 883, Oxford, OX1 9PL, UK
1385 Broadway, 5th Floor, New York, NY 10018, USA
E-mail: info@ospreypublishing.com
www.ospreypublishing.com

OSPREY is a trademark of Osprey Publishing Ltd

First published in Great Britain in 2020

© Osprey Publishing Ltd, 2020

All rights reserved. No part of this publication may be reproduced or transmitted in any form or by any means, electronic or mechanical, including photocopying, recording, or any information storage or retrieval system, without prior permission in writing from the publishers.

A catalog record for this book is available from the British Library.

ISBN: PB 9781472837257; eBook 9781472837264; ePDF 9781472837240; XML 9781472837233

20 21 22 23 24 10 9 8 7 6 5 4 3 2 1

Maps by Bounford.com
3D BEVs by the Black Spot
Index by Alan Rutter
Typeset by PDQ Digital Media Solutions, Bungay, UK
Printed and bound in India by Replika Press Private Ltd.

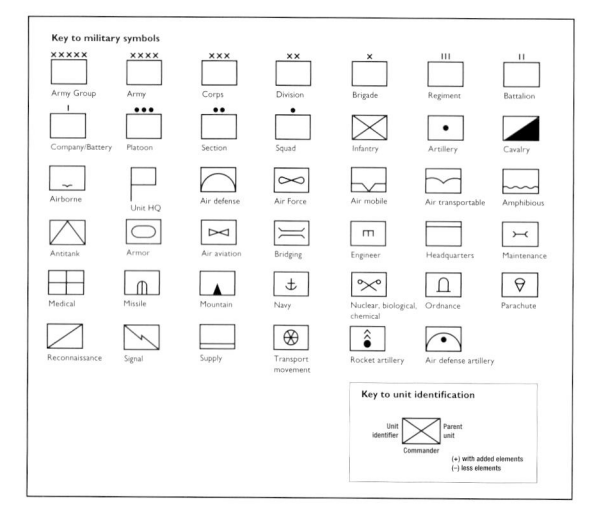

Artist's note

Readers can find out more about the work of illustrator Johnny Shumate at: www.johnnyshumate.com

Osprey Publishing supports the Woodland Trust, the UK's leading woodland conservation charity.

To find out more about our authors and books visit www.ospreypublishing.com. Here you will find extracts, author interviews, details of forthcoming events and the option to sign up for our newsletter.

Author's acknowledgments

This book would not have gotten off the ground without the help of my editors Marcus Cowper and Nikolai Bogdanovic. They helped me extensively to bring the Yalu campaign to completion. My biggest thanks go to my family, especially my wife Cheryl. Without her support, I would never have had the time and opportunity to research and publish. I also want to remember Mei Li who was always there to help me while I researched and wrote.

Dedication

I dedicate this book to my longtime companion and buddy, Lang Lang.

Acronyms

CCF	Communist Chinese Forces
DMZ	Demilitarized Zone
DPRK	Democratic People's Republic of Korea ("North Korea")
EUSAK	Eighth United States Army in Korea
FARELF	Far East Land Forces
FBG	Fighter Bomber Group
FEAF	Far East Air Forces
FEC	Far East Command
JCS	Joint Chiefs of Staff
KATUSA	Korean Augmentations to the US Army
KPA	Korean People's Army (DPRK)
KPN	Korean People's Navy (DPRK)
NATO	North Atlantic Treaty Organization
NAVFE	(US) Naval Forces Far East
PLA	People's Liberation Army (Chinese)
PLAAF	People's Liberation Army Air Force
PLAN	People's Liberation Army Navy
PRC	People's Republic of China
PVA	People's Volunteer Army (Chinese)
ROK	Republic of Korea ("South Korea")
SAC	Strategic Air Command
SCAP	Supreme Commander for the Allied Powers
TF	Task Force
UN	United Nations
UNCOM	United Nations Command
USAF	United States Air Force
USAFFE	United States Army Forces Far East
USMC	United States Marine Corps
USN	United States Navy
USSR	Union of Socialist Soviet Republics

PREVIOUS PAGE
Chinese troops cross the frozen Yalu River.

CONTENTS

ORIGINS OF THE CAMPAIGN 4

CHRONOLOGY 6

OPPOSING COMMANDERS 8
United Nations . Democratic People's Republic of Korea . People's Republic of China

OPPOSING FORCES 12
United Nations . Democratic People's Republic of Korea . People's Republic of China
Orders of battle, October 1950

OPPOSING PLANS 19
United Nations . The DPRK and the PRC

THE CAMPAIGN 24
Crossing the 38th Parallel, October 7–20, 1950 . X Corps' landings at Wonsan and Iwon, October 17–29 . The fall of Pyongyang, October 15–20 . Reaching the Yalu, October 20–23
The Chinese First Phase Offensive, October 19–November 5 . The east: US X Corps pushes north, October 25–November 25 . The Chinese Second Phase Offensive, November 25–December 24
The Chinese Third Phase Offensive, December 31, 1950–January 8, 1951

AFTERMATH 85
UNCOM's counteroffensive, January–April 1951

THE BATTLEFIELD TODAY 91

BIBLIOGRAPHY 94

INDEX 95

ORIGINS OF THE CAMPAIGN

Following the Korean People's Army (KPA) invasion of South Korea in June 1950, Republic of Korea (ROK) units and supporting Eighth US Army (under Lieutenant-General Walton Walker) and United Nations forces (under the overall command of Commander-in-Chief of the United Nations Command General Douglas MacArthur) found themselves penned into the Pusan (Busan) Perimeter in the southeast corner of the peninsula. United Nations forces (including the reactivated US I Corps and IX Corps) massed in Pusan port and used their dominant navy and aviation assets to force a collapse in the attacking KPA units in early September. Operation *Chromite* was launched on September 15, a surprise amphibious assault on the largely undefended city of Inch'on. The highly successful landings were followed by a cautious, 11-day-long, 20-mile advance on the South Korean capital Seoul, which was recaptured on September 25. Within a month of the Inch'on landings, some 135,000 KPA troops had been taken prisoner.

The September 1950 Inch'on amphibious landings were instrumental in forcing Kim Il-Sung's KPA to retreat north of the 38th Parallel. MacArthur took a calculated risk to send the X Corps' 1st Marine Division and 7th Infantry Division behind enemy lines, but it caught the KPA by surprise. (US Marine Corps)

With the recapture of Seoul, questions were raised about the strategic direction of the war. UN forces could advance to the 38th Parallel and halt there, mopping up any remaining KPA forces within ROK territory. This would restore the peninsula to its prewar borders. However, a larger vision was growing at MacArthur's Tokyo headquarters. Could UN forces settle the question of a politically divided Korean peninsula by pushing into Kim Il-Sung's Democratic People's Republic of Korea (DPRK) and advancing to the Chinese border at the Yalu River? The DPRK's defeat appeared imminent. The latter would demonstrate to Mao Zedong's People's Republic of China (PRC) and Josef Stalin's Union of Socialist Soviet Republics (USSR) that the Free World would not tolerate military aggression and there would be a price to pay for any such acts.

Advancing to the Yalu River posed significant risks. The conflict could widen, drawing in both the PRC and the DPRK's principal backer, the USSR. The latter had expanded its military capability, was rapidly developing nuclear weapons and their delivery systems, and in the West was consolidating its grip on Central and Eastern Europe satellite states. Any expansion in the Korean conflict could spark tension not only in Asia, but in Europe and beyond. Given the PRC's focus on the Taiwan Problem and its own internal challenges, a PRC intervention in the DPRK was considered a low risk, certainly by the US military and political leadership. However, the threat posed to Chinese territorial integrity and to its economic reconstruction would prove otherwise.

The Korean War was a major challenge to the fledgling UN. The ROK received political and military support principally from the USA, Great Britain, and several Commonwealth countries in mid-1950, but the political decision-making relationships were shared between several international centers. This was further complicated with military leaders communicating between these centers and the field. Another concern was the fragile civil–military relationship between President Harry S. Truman, as commander-in-chief of America's armed forces, and Commander-in-Chief UNCOM Douglas MacArthur. Even the military chain of command between MacArthur and the Joint Chiefs of Staff, Secretary of the Army, and Army Chief of Staff required extensive staff coordination that resulted in misunderstanding and confrontation. MacArthur himself not only led the UN forces on the peninsula, but also US air, land, and naval forces assigned to the Far East; governed occupied Japan; and oversaw other potential conflict areas such as Taiwan. He also had his own vision, objectives, and goals that differed greatly from those of Truman, other United Nations members, and his subordinates.

ROK soldiers drag a wounded DPRK soldier from a hiding place on the Pohang front, in September 1950. (Bettman/Getty Images)

US 1st Cavalry Division troops fire on retreating KPA soldiers at Waegwan, South Korea in September 1950. (US Army)

CHRONOLOGY

1950

June 25	The KPA invades South Korea.
July 1	The US 24th Infantry Division, spearheaded by Task Force Smith (under Lieutenant-Colonel Charles B. Smith), begins arriving in South Korea to slow the KPA advance and create time for a build-up of US forces.
August 1	Eighth US Army commander Walker establishes the Pusan Perimeter.
September 15	Operation *Chromite* landings at Inch'on.
September 23	UN forces break out of the Pusan Perimeter; the KPA retreats.
September 27	Truman authorizes Commander-in-Chief UNCOM General Douglas MacArthur to cross the 38th Parallel.
September 28	Seoul is recaptured by UN forces.
September 29	US Secretary of Defense George C. Marshall provides detailed guidance to MacArthur allowing him a "free hand" to operate in the DPRK.
September 30	ROK 3rd Division units cross the 38th Parallel on the east coast.
October 1	MacArthur demands that the DPRK surrenders. DPRK premier Kim Il-Sung refuses.
October 3	PRC foreign minister Zhou Enlai informs the Indian ambassador Kavalam M. Panikkar that if the Americans cross the 38th Parallel, the PRC will intervene in the DPRK.
October 10	US 1st Cavalry Division units cross the 38th Parallel. ROK elements take Wonsan.
October 15	MacArthur confers with President Truman at Wake Island. Both believe the PRC will not intervene in the conflict.
October 19	The DPRK capital Pyongyang falls to UN forces. Mao Zedong approves People's Liberation Army (PLA) units to operate in the DPRK under the cover name of the People's Volunteer Army (PVA).
October 20	Walker uses the 187th Airborne Regimental Combat Team to trap KPA units fleeing Pyongyang.
October 25	Chinese PVA units attack ROK troops at Onjong.

October 26	The US 1st Marine Division comes ashore at Wonsan. ROK reconnaissance units reach the Yalu River.
October 29	The US 7th Infantry Division lands at Iwon.
November 1	PVA forces hit Eighth US Army, ROK, and UN forces above the Chongch'on River. A US cavalry battalion is badly mauled by the Chinese.
November 25	PVA forces launch major attacks against Walker's Eighth US Army and Major-General Edward Almond's X Corps.
November 28	MacArthur provokes shock by admitting that the UN faces "an entirely new war."
December 1	Walker consolidates Eighth US Army positions on and south of the Chongch'on River.
December 5	UNCOM forces evacuate Pyongyang.
December 6	Major-General Oliver P. Smith's US 1st Marine Division and remnants of the 31st Regimental Combat Team withdraw from the Chosin Reservoir area and head south to Hungnam.
December 17	Kim Il-Sung is deprived of the command of the KPA by the Chinese.
December 23	Lieutenant-General Walton H. Walker dies in a jeep accident. Lieutenant-General Matthew Ridgway is his replacement.
December 24	US X Corps successfully evacuates from Hungnam and redeploys to support Eighth US Army.

1951

January 1	PVA commander Peng Dehuai launches a third combined PVA/KPA offensive.
January 3	UNCOM forces retreat from Seoul.

OPPOSING COMMANDERS

UNITED NATIONS

US

General Douglas MacArthur, as Supreme Commander for the Allied Powers (SCAP) in occupied Tokyo, had the authority to "exercise supreme command over all land, sea and air forces" throughout Korea. MacArthur also performed as Commander-in-Chief, Far East (CINCFE), for the Far East Command (FEC), in charge of American military forces serving throughout the Western Pacific and Asia. In addition, the Secretary of the Army designated him as Commander, United States Army Forces Far East (USAFFE), leading all Army organizations in theater. When the DPRK invaded the ROK, the UN Security Council authorized defensive operations within the ROK and subsequently requested Washington to name a mission commander. MacArthur was a natural choice, and he gained the title of Commander-in-Chief, United Nations Command (UNCOM). All UNCOM military actions and planning flowed through MacArthur's SCAP headquarters. MacArthur had near total authority, subject to Washington's and the UN's approval, to conduct

General Douglas MacArthur had served 48 years on active duty when he visited troops north of the 38th Parallel on April 3, 1951. His EUSAK commander, Lieutenant-General Matthew Ridgway, directly behind MacArthur, took over from Lieutenant-General Walton Walker following his death in an automobile accident on December 23, 1950. (US Army)

actions in defense of the ROK and against the KPA. However, his command was marred by continual disagreements with President Harry Truman and other key Washington figures over national policy. MacArthur's advocacy of widening the war in April 1951, contrary to official policy, eventually forced Truman to relieve MacArthur.

Lieutenant-General Walton H. Walker, commander of Eighth United States Army in Korea (EUSAK), served as MacArthur's chief land component commander in the peninsula. Walker, a 1912 West Point graduate, served on the US–Mexican border in 1916, in France in 1918, in China during the interwar period, and commanded XX Corps under General George Patton's Third Army during World War II. Walker led EUSAK forces in the successful defense of the Pusan Perimeter, the ensuing breakout, and the drive north across the 38th Parallel. Walker would be killed in a jeep accident on December 23, 1950 at Uijongbu.

Lieutenant-General Matthew Ridgway became commander of Eighth United States Army after Walker's death. Four months later, he would succeed MacArthur as Commander-in-Chief UNCOM. Ridgway was most famous for his service as the 82nd Airborne Division and later the XVIII Airborne Corps commander. Before his assignment to Korea, Ridgway served as the Deputy Chief of Staff of the Army. After the Korean War, he became the Supreme Commander, Allied Forces in Europe and later became the US Army Chief of Staff.

Major-General Edward "Ned" Almond was the commander of the US X Corps. Almond had served in World War I and completed numerous staff and training assignments during the interwar period. During World War II he commanded the 92nd Infantry Division in Italy from 1944 to 1945. Almond was later transferred to the SCAP staff as chief of personnel and eventually became MacArthur's chief of staff. MacArthur appointed him as the X Corps' commander and he took charge of the Inch'on landings. Almond retired in 1953 as Commandant, US Army War College.

Directing the combined UN air forces was **Lieutenant-General George E. Stratemeyer**. After graduating from West Point in 1915, Stratemeyer began his career as an infantryman. He transferred to the fledgling Air Corps in 1920. During World War II, Stratemeyer oversaw a training center, was General Henry "Hap" Arnold's chief of staff, and directed air forces in the China-Burma-India Theater. After the war, he controlled the Air Defense Command. In April 1949, Stratemeyer led the Far East Air Forces (FEAF) in Japan. As FEAF commander, Stratemeyer oversaw air activities against KPA units. He arranged for close air support, interdiction, and strategic bombardment missions for UNCOM forces, and overcame the challenge of consolidating command and control of all theater air forces: US Marine

Major-General Edward "Ned" Almond was MacArthur's chief of staff for FEC and also commanded the X Corps during the Inch'on invasion. Here, he talks to MacArthur aboard the USS *McKinley* while they observe the landings at Inch'on in September 1950. (US Army)

Corps and US Navy carrier aviation commanders were highly suspicious of USAF attempts to control their air assets. Stratemeyer was replaced in May 1951 after suffering a massive heart attack.

Vice Admiral Charles Turner Joy, as Commander, US Naval Forces Far East, supervised all naval activities under MacArthur. Joy served in World War I as a junior officer on the battleship USS *Pennsylvania*. During the interwar period, Joy served on the Chinese Yangtze patrol, destroyer duty, as executive officer on a cruiser, in staff duties, on battleship duty at sea, and was on the staff at a mine depot. During World War II, Joy captained a heavy cruiser and later led a cruiser division. After the war, the US Navy assigned him to China and later to head the Naval Proving Ground at Dahlgren, Virginia. In Korea, Joy directed a naval blockade of the DPRK, transported ground forces and logistics by sea, conducted amphibious operations, and unleashed his carrier airstrike capability against the north.

ROK

Major-General Yu Jae Hung commanded both the ROK II and III Corps in 1950–51. Born in Japan in Aichi province in 1921, he attended a military academy, and went on to serve as a battalion commander in the Imperial Japanese Army during World War II. Following Japan's surrender, he remained in Korea and served in the nascent ROK armed forces. At the outset of the Korean War, Yu Jae Hung was in charge of the ROK 7th Division, and took part in the tactical withdrawal to the Naktong River. In late October 1950, Yu Jae Hung was promoted to Deputy Chief of Staff of the ROK Army and departed the front line for Seoul, handing control of the ROK II Corps to Brigadier-General Paik Sun Yup. Yu Jae Hung was keen to return to the front, however, and on January 9, 1951 was appointed to command the ROK III Corps.

Other nations

Colonel Basil A. Coad commanded the 27th British Commonwealth Brigade. Coad had held several brigade and divisional commands during World War II. At the time of the outbreak of the Korean War, the 27th Infantry Brigade was stationed in Hong Kong as part of Far East Land Forces (FARELF), serving as the UK's Strategic Reserve. Although British forces were heavily committed to the Malayan Emergency at that point, fears over a Chinese threat to Hong Kong forced a British intervention in the war in early August 1950. The brigade (consisting almost entirely of infantry) arrived in the ROK on August 29 and joined the defense of the Pusan Perimeter. It then covered the flank of the main US advance on Seoul, before being attached to the US 24th Infantry Division and then subsequently Eighth US Army. The 3rd Battalion, Royal Australian Regiment arrived in Korea on September 28 and was attached to the brigade. The brigade was renamed the 27th British Commonwealth Brigade at this point.

Brigadier-General Tahsin Yazici commanded the Turkish Brigade during the Korean War. In June 1950, the Republic of Turkey was among the first to respond to the UN request for military aid to the ROK by sending a 5,000-strong brigade, consisting of three infantry battalions, an artillery battalion, and auxiliary units. Attached to the US 25th Infantry Division, the brigade was heavily involved in the fighting around Kunu-ri, November 27–29, 1950. Yazici (who did not speak English) earned a Silver Star for his leadership.

DEMOCRATIC PEOPLE'S REPUBLIC OF KOREA

Selected by Premier Kim Il-Sung, **Marshal Nam Il** served as the Chief of Staff for the General Headquarters, KPA. Born in the Soviet Union in 1925, Nam graduated from a military academy in Smolensk, and joined the Soviet Red Army after Germany initiated Operation *Barbarossa*. According to a 1951 EUSAK study, Nam served as a divisional commander at Stalingrad, alongside Kim Il-Sung. After the war, Nam went to Soviet-occupied North Korea, which became the DPRK in 1948. He retained many of his Soviet army contacts and maintained a close friendship with Kim. As the KPA I Corps commander, Nam crossed the 38th Parallel on June 25, 1950 into the ROK. Nam was appointed to command all KPA forces and would remain in this role until the July 1953 armistice, in which he played a major negotiation role. Nam died in 1976 in an alleged automobile accident; there is speculation that his death was due to an internal power struggle with Kim Il-Sung.

The DPRK leader Kim Il-Sung signs the Korean Armistice Agreement in July 1953. To Kim's right, handing him the agreement, is Marshal Nam Il. (Sovfoto/Universal Images Group/Getty Images)

PEOPLE'S REPUBLIC OF CHINA

Marshal Peng Dehuai led the sanctioned People's Volunteer Army force of 380,000 soldiers fighting in Korea. Peng was not Chairman Mao Zedong's first choice to head the PVA, but the ill health suffered by Lin Biao led to Peng's appointment. Peng was an ardent advocate of the PRC's entry into the Korean War. Born in 1898, Peng began his military career in a Nationalist Kuomintang-leaning warlord's army. He served under the Kuomintang banner until 1928, when he became a communist. Peng fought his former comrades until 1937, when both the Kuomintang and communists joined forces to fight Japan. After World War II, Peng fought the American-backed Kuomintang until Chiang Kai-shek and his supporters fled to Taiwan in 1949. Peng took part in the 1953 armistice negotiations and signed the ceasefire document halting combat operations between communist and UNCOM forces. After the war, Peng served as the PRC's Defense Minister, before falling from grace with Mao. He died in poor health in 1974.

Mao Zedong selected Marshal Peng Dehuai to command and direct PVA operations in the DPRK. Although he succeeded in pushing MacArthur out of the North, his forces sustained heavy casualties in the effort. He failed to produce an effective offensive to push UNCOM completely out of Korea. Peng, second to the left, is shown here meeting the USSR Premier Nikita Khrushchev (far right). (Wikimedia Commons)

OPPOSING FORCES

UNITED NATIONS

US infantry divisions operating in Korea each had three infantry regiments, a battalion of armor, divisional artillery, and organic support. An infantry division numbered approximately 18,800 men. Each infantry regiment consisted of three infantry battalions, an armor company, a heavy weapons company, and staff. The divisional support personnel included headquarters staff, engineer, medical, reconnaissance, signal, military police, supply, and aviation assets. By 1950, the US Army was struggling with funding issues as it strove to replace World War II-era equipment. Given the mounting threat to Western Europe from the Soviet Union, NATO-assigned US Army formations received the latest and best equipment. Eighth US Army largely employed obsolete equipment, for example the M-24 Chafee light tank, which was outmatched by the KPA's T-34 tanks. The heavier World War II M-4 Sherman was better matched, but was still vulnerable to a T-34 hit.

During the early Korean War fighting, American armor was too light to counter Soviet-made T-34 tanks. As the war progressed, the US Army began to field tanks that could counter the T-34. The M-26 Pershing medium tank's 90mm round could penetrate the T-34's armor, and its heavier armor protected its crew better than the M-24. US Marines also used the M-26. (US Marine Corps)

Initially, the US Marine Corps (USMC) had sent the 1st Provisional Marine Brigade from Camp Pendleton, California to help defend Korea. The USMC had been cut following World War II, and it now required legislation to rebuild it. President Truman authorized two fully mobilized divisions. Camp Lejeune's 2nd Marine Division formed the base for rebuilding Camp Pendleton's depleted 1st Marine Division. Eventually, the 1st Marine Division deployed and fought with the 1st, 5th, and 7th Regimental Combat teams with appropriate support units (armor, engineer, ordnance, signal, medical, amphibious tractor, and others). The 11th Marine Regiment provided artillery and rocket fire support. Depending on the units available and distance from the ocean, the 1st Marine Division could request naval gunfire support from offshore vessels. On October 8, 1950, 1st Marine Division had 25,770 men assigned. The Marines also employed 2,159 KATUSA-like equivalents. Later, due to combat and weather casualties at the Chosin Reservoir, US Army personnel served as replacements.

Aviation

Before the outbreak of the Korean War, the USAF's FEAF consisted of the Fifth, Ninth, and Twentieth air forces. Fifth Air Force was predominantly assigned to Korea, but the USAF also directed a Twentieth Air Force B-29 group (on Okinawa) to conduct strategic bombardment missions. Strategic Air Command would later assign additional B-29 groups to FEAF operations.

At the war's start, Fifth Air Force units were based in Japan. This limited the range and endurance of tactical aircraft, affecting close air support and interdiction missions. USAF F-80s, F-82s, F-51s, B-26s, and C-54s made herculean efforts to attack KPA vehicles, strafe convoys, and transport supplies and personnel. By November 1950, FEAF crews flew from several sites within Korea. At K-14, north of Seoul, the 51st Fighter-Interceptor Group (16th Fighter Squadron, 25th Fighter Squadron, and 80th Fighter-Bomber Squadron) flew F-86F and F-80Cs. The 8th Fighter-Bomber Group, also stationed at K-14, contributed the 35th and 36th Fighter-Bomber squadrons with F-80s. K-2, east of Taegu, was home to the 49th Fighter-Bomber Group with its F-80-armed 7th, 8th, and 9th Fighter squadrons. The 49th Fighter-Bomber Group was the first jet unit to fly from South Korea. Sharing K-2 was the 543rd Tactical Support Group with its 8th and 162nd Tactical Reconnaissance squadrons. On Korea's southeast coast was K-3 with the 35th Fighter-Interceptor Group composed of the 39th and 40th Fighter squadrons that flew F-80s; this later switched to longer-ranged F-51s. Also at K-3 was No. 77 Squadron, Royal Australian Air Force, flying F-51s. K-9, southwest of Pusan, hosted the 18th Fighter-Bomber Group with its 12th and 67th Fighter-Bomber squadrons, which, like the 35th Fighter-Interceptor Group, exchanged their F-80s for F-51s. Later, No. 2 Squadron, South African Air Force, flying F-51s, joined the 18th Fighter-Bomber Group. As UNCOM units pushed rapidly northward, some Fifth Air Force units moved to K-24, east of Pyongyang. As the war continued, new units, such as the 27th Fighter-Escort Group with F-84s, flew from K-2, to supplement other FEAF units.

In August 1950, the ROK government approved a proposal to fill vacant manpower in US Army units with up to 8,600 Korean personnel. Later, the limit was raised to no more than 40,000, but US units could only employ 23,000 at a given time. By September 1950, the US 7th Infantry Division alone had 8,000 Korean Augmentation to the United States Army (KATUSA) troops, and the US 3rd Infantry Division had about 6,000. As US training programs improved, the KATUSA manpower was released to ROK units. (US Army)

ABOVE LEFT
A napalm bomb strikes a DPRK supply depot. The first napalm bombs were dropped on Tinian Island in 1944, and by the time of the Korean War their use was widespread. UNCOM air forces dropped over 110,000kg of napalm during the conflict, mostly in the form of the M-47 napalm bomb and the M-74 incendiary bomb, using both high-altitude and tactical bombers. (US Air Force)

ABOVE RIGHT
UNCOM air assets could conduct strategic bombardment, interdiction, reconnaissance, or close air support missions. A major source of these came from Task Force 77. Here, US Navy AD Skyraiders, from the USS *Valley Forge* attack squadron VA-55, launch 5in. rockets at a KPA position. (US Navy)

The B-29 strategic bombing campaign against the DPRK took its toll on the KPA's logistics: B-29 aircraft destroyed most of Pyongyang's limited industry within days. These actions released the B-29s to conduct other missions. After the Chinese intervention, these B-29s switched to targeting the Yalu River bridges to interfere with PVA supply and troop movements into the DPRK. These B-29s, now closer to Chinese air bases on the Yalu border, faced a potent threat: the MIG-15. The MIG-15 outclassed the F-80, but the recently developed F-86 was a better match, and several Fifth Air Force units converted to it.

Fifth Air Force units in Japan supported other military activities throughout the Korean peninsula. At least four Troop Carrier groups (1st Provisional, 314th, 374th, and 437th) could send in rapid reinforcements and supplies, and evacuate wounded personnel. Japan also served as home base for the 3rd (B-26), 98th (B-29 from Strategic Air Command), and 452nd (activated USAF Reserve B-26 unit) Bomb Groups. Reconnaissance aircraft, rescue, and other units assigned for the defense of Japan also supported UNCOM's Korean operations.

B-29 crews are briefed by a 98th Bombardment Group intelligence officer on their target over Sinuiju, at the mouth of the Yalu River. Sinuiju was defended by heavy antiaircraft artillery concentrations, and later in the war by MIG-15s from Antung in the PRC. These crews flew out of Yokota Air Base in November 1950. (US Air Force)

The 1st Marine Aircraft Wing supplied aircraft to the 1st Provisional Marine Brigade. Marine squadrons VMF-343 (F-4U), VMF-214 (F-4U), VMF(N)-313 (F-7F), and VMO-6 (OY-2 and HO3S-1 helicopters) flew under Marine Aircraft Group-33. Both VMF-214 and VMF-343 initially flew off carriers, while VMF(N)-313 operated from Itazuke, Japan. VMO-6 personnel operated from Pusan.

Naval

The US Naval Forces Far East (NAVFE) controlled all American and UNCOM-assigned naval units. NAVFE-assigned ships operated in theater on a rotational basis. Although US Navy ships dominated operations at sea, nine other countries sent naval forces to Korea. NAVFE had several roles and missions aside from fighting in Korea, including patrolling the Western Pacific, protecting Japan, and acting as a deterrent against the PRC and the USSR. UNCOM could employ NAVFE to provide amphibious support, transport supplies and personnel, deliver naval gunfire, blockade the DPRK, intercept enemy supply ships, and conduct carrier air missions.

The major operational NAVFE command was the US Seventh Fleet based in the Philippines. Its major strike capability was TF 77, which operated fast aircraft carriers, battleships, and cruisers. TF 77 led the Inch'on landings, but also conducted extensive bombing of the Yalu bridges. TF 77 carriers operating during the Yalu campaign included the *Boxer*, *Leyte*, *Princeton*, *Valley Forge*, *Philippine Sea*, *Bataan*, *Barioko*, *Badoeng Strait*, and *Sicily* and Escort Carrier Group (Task Group 96.8). *Princeton* was a typical carrier: from May to December 1950 it operated four fighter squadrons (VF-51 and VF-52 with F9Fs, and VF-53 and VF-54 flying F4Us), an attack squadron with AD Skyraiders, and detachments from different squadrons that included helicopters and night-fighters. Washington also reactivated four Iowa-class 16in.-gun battleships for Korea to supplement naval gunfire support to its deployed cruisers.

NAVFE also controlled Amphibious, Far East (TF 90), UN Blockading and Escort Force (TF 95), the ROK Navy, and other support activities. Commonwealth naval units were also sent to the theater. The Royal Navy operated aircraft carriers during the Korean conflict, notably HMS *Theseus*. Canada, Australia, and New Zealand also operated ships to include a light carrier (Australia), light cruisers, destroyers, and frigates.

BELOW LEFT
The Royal Marines 41 (Independent) Commando, under the command of Lieutenant-Colonel Douglas B. Drysdale, served under the US 1st Marine Division. On arrival in Korea, the Commandos were issued American winter uniforms and weapons but retained their green berets, battle dress, and boots. The Royal Marines (shown here planting demolition charges on a railway line) conducted several coastal raids and served as conventional infantry. At the Chosin Reservoir, Drysdale led a 900-strong combined Commando, US, and ROK unit called Task Force Drysdale. (US Navy)

BELOW RIGHT
UNCOM forces held the advantage in mechanized forces, air power, naval forces, and a vast logistical system. However, victory of defeat lay in the hands of the individual soldier or marine. (US Marine Corps)

DEMOCRATIC PEOPLE'S REPUBLIC OF KOREA

Infantry divisions dominated the KPA's military structure, but an armored brigade was also available. The KPA initially sent some 135,000 men across the border. Many were veterans who had served with the communist Chinese, fought the Japanese as guerrillas, or joined the Soviet Army. Beijing and Moscow supplied the KPA with small arms, artillery, tanks, and munitions along with training. DPRK officials organized their forces on a Soviet model. At the outbreak of the Korean War, the KPA consisted of seven infantry divisions, a tank brigade (later expanded into a division), an independent infantry regiment, a motorcycle regiment, three reserve infantry divisions, and a border constabulary. Each infantry division consisted of 11,000 troops organized into three regiments.

After the Inch'on landings and the breakout from the Pusan Perimeter, the tide of war changed for the DPRK. With MacArthur on the offensive and the KPA in retreat, North Korean manpower requirements exceeded available resources, and young boys were often drafted in to fight. These KPA prisoners, captured in the Singdang-dong neighborhood of Seoul, are being interrogated. (US Army)

At the start of the war, the KPA consisted of three corps: I Corps (1st, 3rd, 4th, and 6th divisions plus the 105th Armored Brigade), II Corps (2nd, 5th, and 7th divisions), and III Corps (10th, 13th, and 15th divisions)—the latter serving as the reserve. In terms of armor, the KPA contained some 150 T-34 tanks; most were lost during the summer of 1950 as UNCOM firepower increased. By October 1950, only 25,000 to 30,000 invasion-assigned soldiers re-crossed the 38th Parallel back into the DPRK. Those DPRK troops trapped in South Korea could only conduct limited guerrilla actions. New infantry divisions—the 18th, 31st, and 32nd—were formed.

The Korean People's Air Force (KPAF) had 93 Il-10 fighters (1st Assault Aviation Regiment), 79 Yak-9 fighters (1st Fighter Aviation Regiment), and the 1st Combined Aviation Regiment (40–50 trainers, transports, and other aircraft). The KPAF was badly mauled early in the war, and as the KPA withdrew north, it reformed in China.

The Korean People's Navy (KPN) maintained a 45-vessel coastal patrol and coast guard, which was wiped out at the war's start.

PEOPLE'S REPUBLIC OF CHINA

In the wake of the Chinese crossing of the Yalu River, Beijing announced that only "volunteers" (part of the People's Vounteer Army) had joined the fight, not the People's Liberation Army, providing political cover for the intervention. MacArthur's staff referred to such units in Korea as Communist Chinese Forces (CCF). Approximately 380,000 Chinese combat and support personnel crossed into the DPRK in October 1950, under the command of the Fourth Field Army in Mukden. Initially, MacArthur's intelligence officers estimated the total Chinese personnel at only 34,500 after their intervention.

Initially, four essentially corps-sized units (but called armies) were sent to Korea; this soon grew to six—38th, 39th, 40th, 42nd, 50th, and 66th. Each Chinese corps equivalent contained three to four infantry divisions. Each division contained 4,000 to 8,000 men with authorizations from 8,000 to 10,000 soldiers.

The PVA lacked modern equipment and weaponry. Its soldiers fought with a mixture of captured World War II-era American and Japanese weapons alongside Soviet ones. This complicated logistics. In addition, the size of the PLA—about 5 million personnel—made standardizing its training and equipment difficult. Infantry divisions lacked field artillery and fire support was usually provided by a limited number of mortars and howitzers. The Chinese also lacked armor, transportation, medical supplies and personnel, anti-aircraft weapons, and basic supplies. The PVA's divisions had to rely on night marches, camouflage, surprise, and mass attacks to overcome American technical and materiel superiority. Although their initial advance shocked UNCOM, the Chinese had a difficult time sustaining their offensives throughout the war.

The PLA Air Force (PLAAF) was organized along Soviet lines with air divisions and regiments. Chinese pilots flew a number of Soviet aircraft, including the LA-9, LA-10, YAK-9, TU-2, and MIG-15. The PLAAF oversaw the combined KPA and Chinese air operations under the United Air Force from November 1, the same day PLAAF MIG-15s entered combat. American intelligence sources estimated PLAAF strength at 650 aircraft in December 1950. This total expanded to 1,050 by June 1951. Increasingly, the PLAAF added MIG-15s to contest air superiority over the DPRK, as USAF and USN aircraft conducted strategic bombardment, interdiction, and close air support missions. Several Soviet pilots deployed with the PLAAF and shot down UN aircraft. The PLAAF used bases in Manchuria near Antung and north of the Yalu River, as the US Fifth Air Force was not permitted to attack sites in China.

The PLA Navy played no major role in the conflict.

Chinese soldiers of the PVA prepare to depart for the DPRK in October 1950. Note the lack of uniformity in dress and equipment. (Bettman/Getty Images)

ORDERS OF BATTLE, OCTOBER 1950

UNITED NATIONS

In October 1950, UNCOM ground combat strength numbered 198,211 men, with 113,494 from the US Army and Marine Corps. ROK strength was 81,644 personnel.

EIGHTH US ARMY

(Lieutenant-General Walton Walker)
(EUSAK divisions included attached Korean Augmentations to the US Army—KATUSA—troops, to fill gaps in US manpower.)
I Corps (Major-General Frank W. Milburn)
(activated at Fort Bragg, North Carolina, August 2, 1950)
US 1st Cavalry Division
US 24th Infantry Division
ROK 1st Infantry Division
27th British Commonwealth Brigade
US IX Corps (Major-General John B. Coulter)
(became operational September 23, 1950)
US 2nd Infantry Division
US 25th Infantry Division

US X CORPS (INDEPENDENT)

(Major-General Edward Almond)
US 7th Infantry Division
US 1st Marine Division

ROK

ROK I Corps (assigned to US X Corps c. October 20, 1950)
ROK II Corps
ROK III Corps

DEMOCRATIC PEOPLE'S REPUBLIC OF KOREA

KOREAN PEOPLE'S ARMY

(Marshal Nam Il)
I Corps
1st Division
3rd Division
4th Division
6th Division
105th Armored Brigade
II Corps
2nd Division
5th Division
7th Division
III Corps
10th Division
13th Division
15th Division

PEOPLE'S REPUBLIC OF CHINA

PEOPLE'S VOLUNTEER ARMY: NORTH EAST FRONTIER FORCE

(Marshal Peng Dehuai—commander and commissar)
(On November 10, 1950, the PLA Ninth Army entered Korea to reinforce PVA units east of the Taebaek Mountains. The Ninth consisted of the 20th, 26th, and 27th armies and was heavily involved in the fighting at the Chosin Reservoir.)
38th Army
(Commander: Liang Xingchu. Commissar: Liu Xiyuan)
112th Division
113th Division
114th Division
39th Army
(Commander: Wu Xinquan. Commissar: Xu Binzhou)
115th Division
116th Division
117th Division
40th Army
(Commander: Wen Yucheng. Commissar: Yuan Shengping)
118th Division
119th Division
120th Division
42nd Army
(Commander: Wu Ruilin. Commissar: Zhou Biao)
124th Division
125th Division
126th Division
50th Army
(Commander: Zeng Zesheng. Commissar Xu Wenlie)
148th Division
149th Division
150th Division
66th Army
(Commander: Xiao Xinhuai. Commissar: Wang Zifeng)
196th Division
197th Division
198th Division
Artillery
(Commander: Kuang Yumin. Commissar: Qiu Chuangcheng)
1st Artillery Division
2nd Artillery Division
8th Artillery Division
1st Antiaircraft Artillery Regiment
Engineer
4th Engineer Regiment
6th Engineer Regiment
Logistics
1st Detachment
2nd Detachment

OPPOSING PLANS

UNITED NATIONS

As UNCOM units neared the DPRK border, the war appeared to be moving toward a DPRK defeat. The UN original mandate to defend and restore the ROK following Pyongyang's invasion seemed settled. Should UNCOM forces stop at the 38th Parallel or push on into the DPRK?

A major victory over the communists seemed likely. Critics of US President Truman had accused him of losing China to the communists when it became the PRC on October 1, 1949. Earlier, on August 29, 1949, the USSR had successfully detonated an atomic bomb, ending America's nuclear monopoly. Moreover, Moscow had challenged the West with a blockade of Berlin and supported a communist movement in Greece. Now, with UNCOM's apparent victory, Truman was on the verge of altering the strategic perception of a string of unbroken communist successes. A drive north and the KPA's destruction would mean the fall of the DPRK. Having the capability and opportunity to crush the KPA now allowed Truman to make good his demand, on September 1, 1950, for a "free, independent, and united" nation, and would prove that he was not "soft" on communism. It might also help Truman in the upcoming November congressional elections. A free, unified Korea would also allow the United States to control critical supplies of coal, hydroelectric power, and other raw materials to China.

Truman assumed an UNCOM drive north would be contested by neither the PRC nor the USSR. However, a Chinese or Soviet intervention might lead to a broadening of the conflict. The British government was especially cautious about crossing the 38th Parallel, fearing the move might signal a drastic change in the war. If the UN, and the United States in particular, became bogged down in Korea, then the Soviets might see an opportunity to strike at Western Europe.

Truman's State Department had additional concerns. The 1948 Truman Doctrine to stop communist expansion was based on containment. Washington sought to ring the USSR with free countries that boasted economic growth coupled with security cooperation. A drive to Pyongyang and beyond might negate this strategy. The Chairman of

President Harry S. Truman approved MacArthur's offensive into the DPRK. Truman would later sign a national emergency order on December 16, 1950 that increased the defense budget and expanded manpower for the US armed forces. (National Archives)

This T-34 was caught on a bridge while retreating north of Suwon (20km south of the ROK capital), as the EUSAK pushed toward Seoul. (US Army)

the Joint Chiefs of Staff (JCS) General Omar Bradley urged caution and counselled Truman to proceed slowly. His concern was that a conflict expansion might evolve into a total nuclear war, but with MacArthur's UNCOM advancing unimpeded the criticism was muted. It would still require a new UN mandate to continue military operations into the north since the UN Security Council decision of June 27, 1950 limited UN units to repelling the DPRK attack and restoring the original border.

Discussions between MacArthur and the US JCS about entering the DPRK were not new. On July 13, 1950, the ROK President Syngman Rhee had declared that the DPRK attack southward had permanently destroyed the 38th Parallel as a border. The next day, MacArthur and the JCS mooted the possibility of driving the invading DPRK forces from the south and occupying the entire Korean peninsula. If the PRC did intervene, the USAF always had the option of threatening Chinese targets with the atomic bomb. Truman directed the JCS to study the issue. By early August, the UN Commission on Korea agreed that a combined, democratic Korea was a desirable objective. This led to American, British, and French efforts to approve a UN General Assembly mandate to create a single independent Korea.

The US National Security Council completed a study that recommended crossing the 38th Parallel and seizing the DPRK. However, the NSC did caveat their conclusions by stating that UNCOM should only proceed if the PRC or USSR did not commit ground forces to the conflict. The JCS notified MacArthur of the study's findings the day UNCOM forces landed at Inch'on, September 15.

On September 27, MacArthur received authorization by JCS Chairman General Omar Bradley to proceed north of the original border and destroy the KPA, unless Beijing or Moscow intervened or threatened to do so in

The Taebeck Mountains run through the center of the Korean Peninsula. The steep ridges and few roads made mutual support and logistics between UNCOM's EUSAK in the west and X Corps in the east difficult at best. (US Air Force)

the conflict, at which point MacArthur should move to the defensive. If the PRC attacked, he was to continue fighting as long as he could resist. MacArthur was also advised to only use ROK units near the Chinese and Soviet borders. Bradley cautioned MacArthur not to send UNCOM forces into China or the USSR. MacArthur responded that he would first demand Kim Il-Sung's unconditional surrender. If Pyongyang failed to comply, MacArthur would move into the DPRK.

The US Secretary of Defense George C. Marshall, with Truman's concurrence, provided an endorsement of total support to MacArthur on September 29 by stating that he was free to move north and take any actions "strategically and tactically" that he deemed necessary. MacArthur's response was "[u]nless and until the enemy capitulates, I regard all of Korea open for our military operations." The UN General Assembly later passed a resolution to authorize its forces in theater to create a "unified, independent, and democratic" Korea on October 7. MacArthur was now free to direct UN forces to breach the 38th Parallel.

EUSAK commander Lieutenant-General Walker tasked his I Corps (1st Cavalry Division, 24th Infantry Division, ROK 1st Division, and 27th British Commonwealth Brigade) with the capture of the DPRK capital Pyongyang. To the east, the ROK II Corps (ROK 6th, 7th, and 8th divisions) would hold Korea's central region and protect I Corps' right flank. These ROK units would deploy between Uijongbu and Ch'unch'on, forming a line about 35 miles long. EUSAK's IX Corps would deploy south of the Han River, and their mission was to secure communications lines in Walker's rear. The ROK I Corps held positions to the left on the east coast. Meanwhile, the ROK 3rd and Capital divisions would advance and take Wonsan, and the independent US X Corps would make an amphibious landing at Wonsan, drive north, link up with EUSAK, and attack Pyongyang from the rear and flanks, encircling the KPA. EUSAK would strike first, followed by X Corps' landing at Wonsan a week later.

However, the Taebaek mountain range separated the EUSAK and X Corps. If either force was struck, then one could not easily support the other. The existing east–west mountain routes were poor, and limited UNCOM's ability to shift units or provide logistical support either rapidly or efficiently. In addition, the necessary elements of the US Navy would have to transit from the west to the east coast of the peninsula in order to execute X Corps' Wonsan landing. If the DPRK mined or wrecked Wonsan's port, then the US Navy would need to find an alternate landing site. Another major problem for MacArthur was that he had created two separate commands in EUSAK and X Corps. MacArthur initially intended on only sending ROK units forward to the Yalu River, with US and other UN forces remaining in the rear some 50–100 miles south of the river.

Regardless of the UNCOM plan, ROK President Syngman Rhee had independently determined on permanently defeating the DPRK. Rhee had made plans to move ROK troops north of the 38th Parallel and on to the Chinese border. On September 29, the president ordered the ROK 3rd Division to enter DPRK territory, soon followed by the ROK Capital Division.

South Korea's President Syngman Rhee (left) is shown here with Vice Admiral Sohn Won Il (right), Chief of Naval Operations of the Republic of Korea, in September 1950. When the Republic of Korea government was established on August 15, 1948, Sohn oversaw the transformation of the Korean Coast Guard into the Republic of Korea Navy, and as a result is considered its founding father. (Hank Walker/ The LIFE Picture Collection/ Getty Images)

THE DPRK AND THE PRC

The leadership of the DPRK was well aware that the KPA was facing almost certain destruction. Its sole hope for survival was to withdraw north into the mountainous central region where it could fight a defensive war whilst regrouping. Premier Kim Il-Sung appealed to both the PRC and USSR to provide massive amounts of aid to replace materiel losses and to resupply his battered military, to continue the fight for survival. As it was pushed back northward, the KPA continued to incur huge casualties and lost communications between units and their leadership.

Both Beijing and Moscow had celebrated the early victories that the KPA had won over the ROK and UN forces in June 1950. By the end of September, however, Seoul had been recaptured and UNCOM was focusing on the 38th Parallel. The communist gamble to expand permanently into South Korea had apparently failed. For Mao, this meant a potentially permanent Free World presence on his border. The new PRC had just won a long, bitter fight against the Nationalists, who still threatened a potential invasion of the mainland from Taiwan. Britain maintained its colony in Hong Kong. France controlled Indochina. Washington possessed bases on Guam, Okinawa, and Japan. The US Navy's Seventh Fleet plied the South and East China seas. The loss of the DPRK would add another access point for the West to attack the PRC, and would mark a definitive reversal of the communist revolution in the East. Mao could face challenges domestically and internationally concerning his failure to stop the imperialists from establishing a base on China's doorstop, and he understood that action was necessary. Any Chinese intervention to intervene in the DPRK required the approval of the Chinese Politburo, military aid from the USSR, and a redeployment of forces that might affect defensive preparations against potential attacks along China's periphery.

The CIA received a September 30 report from US ambassador to Moscow Alan Kirk that the Chinese leadership had decided to intervene once UN forces crossed the 38th Parallel. Kirk stated that Beijing speculated that an American move north was a prelude to attack into Manchuria and China with a goal of restoring Chiang Kai-shek to power. Kirk asserted that he did not find this evidence convincing. On October 1, Chinese Foreign Minister Zhou Enlai, in a speech celebrating the PRC's first anniversary, declared that China would not stand by while the "imperialists wantonly invade the territory of our neighbor."

On October 3, 1950 Zhou Enlai warned India's ambassador to China, Kavalam Madhava Pannikkar, that if MacArthur crossed the 38th Parallel, China would intervene militarily. However, they would not attack if ROK divisions crossed alone. The CIA dismissed the report, believing Beijing would have intervened earlier if it wished to do so, when UNCOM forces were being pushed south.

Border security was not the only aspect behind Beijing's rationale to intervene. Mao and Stalin had supported the invasion of the ROK, and turning their back on the DPRK at this moment of crisis risked worldwide political embarrassment. If Mao wanted to become the Asian communist hegemon, then he had to move now to save the DPRK. If he did not act promptly, Stalin might do so, and this would diminish greatly the perception of Mao in Asia for decades, or permanently.

Mao had to limit the war. Before the KPA marched south in June, Mao had decided not to invade Taiwan and create a new front. Still, attacking the UN forces chanced a major conflict with the Free World. Both Pyongyang and Beijing understood that a roused USA might deploy additional units, crush Chinese troops, and drive north into the PRC. As early as July 2, Zhou Enlai informed the Soviet ambassador that the PRC could mass three field armies (corps equivalents), around 120,000 men, at the border and intervene if Pyongyang failed to capture South Korea and their attack faltered. By July 19, the PRC gathered 320,000 men in northeast China, although MacArthur's staff speculated these only amounted to around 115,000 Chinese soldiers at that time. Mao suggested that these soldiers would support the DPRK if the UN succeeded in countering the KPA's invasion.

Mao had been confident that the KPA would overcome the UN forces, but this was based on three faulty assumptions. First, he believed the USA was overstretched in its commitments stretching from Germany to Korea. Second, American logistical lines had to cross the Pacific Ocean and could not adequately support MacArthur's command. Third, US fighting power appeared diminished. However, Washington's willingness to deploy forces to Korea demonstrated America's resolve to mobilize, supply, and fight a threat worldwide. Moreover, before the outbreak of hostilities, Mao had counted on the USSR supplying air support to the DPRK, but Stalin reneged on this.

Mao lacked the logistics and airpower to support major operations against the UN without the USSR's support, but he still chose to deploy massive land forces to fight MacArthur. Beijing hoped that sending in several armies would allow Peng Dehuai to smash UNCOM forces in the coming winter weather before the reinforcements could be deployed. On October 1, Kim Il-Sung requested a Chinese military intervention. Mao wanted Soviet airpower and more time to deploy, but Stalin again hedged. Mao was compelled to act, and decided to shift Chinese forces into the DPRK no later than October 19 without Stalin's guarantee of air support.

The Chinese planned on springing the trap on MacArthur. In their First Phase Offensive, they would strike the EUSAK in November. This attack served to gauge UNCOM combat capability and warn UNCOM of further actions. If MacArthur persisted, then additional field armies would be sent into the DPRK. Under a Second Phase Offensive, combined Chinese and DPRK divisions would hit the ROK II Corps and block any retreat avenues for EUSAK troops. In addition, Chinese units would concentrate against the EUSAK to eject its forces from Pyongyang. Once the KPA–PVA forces had pushed UNCOM forces south of Pyongyang, they would be in a position to secure outright victory.

The 19th Bombardment Group conducted their B-29 missions over DPRK from Okinawa after moving from Guam. Once UNCOM forces had pushed the KPA out of the ROK, the 19th targeted strategic sites in the DPRK, including industrial and hydroelectric facilities, bridges, marshalling yards, supply centers, artillery and troop positions, barracks, port facilities, and airfields. (US Air Force)

THE CAMPAIGN

CROSSING THE 38TH PARALLEL, OCTOBER 7–20, 1950

The 38th Parallel North formed the border between North and South Korea prior to the Korean War. Colonel Charles Bonesteel, a US Army officer serving on the JCS, had proposed this line as a boundary for Moscow and Washington to divide Korea at World War II's end. North of this border, Japanese forces would surrender to the Soviets, while those to the south would surrender to US forces. This line also divided Korea into approximately equal halves.

Before ordering his command across the border, MacArthur called on Kim to surrender and release any UNCOM prisoners through a radio broadcast on October 1. If no response were forthcoming, then UNCOM would seek out and destroy any KPA forces wherever they were located. Kim Il-Sung rejected the call to surrender.

US Army and USMC troops were armed with many World War II-era weapons, but some weapons, such as the M1918 Browning Automatic Rifle shown being fired here, were even older. The M1918 fired a .30-06 round from a standard 20-round magazine. (US Army)

EUSAK crosses the 38th Parallel, October 7–26, 1950

EUSAK's operations order for the crossing of the 38th Parallel was issued on October 5, 1950, but no date was given for launching the attack. The drive to capture the DPRK capital Pyongyang was set to begin. UNCOM forces expected to encounter stiff PKA opposition, based around three southern-facing defensive lines (identified by ROK intelligence) stretching across the peninsula, with a particular concentration around Pyongyang itself. These defensive lines comprised gun emplacements and pillboxes, trench systems, and barbed-wire obstacles, and incorporated natural defensive features.

The KPA had activated several new divisions, to bolster those that had fought around Seoul. In the west of the peninsula, the KPA 9th and 17th divisions defended the Kumch'on–Namch'onjom area north of Kaesong. To the west of these units, elements of the KPA 43rd Division defended the Yesong River crossing site west of Kaesong, while the rest of the division defended the coastal area beyond the city. Elements of the 17th Armored Division were also present in this sector facing EUSAK forces.

The lead elements of the US 1st Cavalry Division crossed the 38th Parallel in the afternoon of October 7, with further elements following during the night of October 8. The following day, October 9, Major-General Hobart Gay ordered his division to cross the Parallel and begin fighting its way north. That same day, MacArthur reissued his demand for the DPRK to surrender, only for it to be met with a further rejection by Kim Il-Sung on October 10.

In the center of US 1st Cavalry Division's advance, progress along the heavily mined main highway was slow. On October 12, halfway to Kumch'on, an enemy strongpoint comprising armor, self-propelled guns, and antiaircraft weapons was encountered.

On the right of the division, the 5th Cavalry Regiment (which crossed the Parallel on the morning of October 10) also encountered delays. Having captured the hills dominating the road on both sides just above the Parallel,

Direct and indirect fire support artillery provided a vital combat multiplier for MacArthur's forces. A typical US Army infantry division could call on 54 105mm howitzers (such as the one shown here) and 18 155mm howitzers. (Department of Defense)

it was halted at a KPA-held ridgeline 15 miles northeast of Kaesong. The 5th Cavalry cleared the ridge during the afternoon of October 12.

Following the advance of the 5th Cavalry was the 27th British Commonwealth Brigade, which included armored elements. Gay had planned for the brigade to move northwest through the mountains to envelop PKA forces, but the roads proved to be impassable.

The ROK 1st Division, supported by tanks from 6th Medium Tank Battalion, began to advance in a northwesterly direction, on the right flank of the US 1st Cavalry Division, on a separate road to the US 5th Cavalry Regiment that would converge in the approach to Pyongyang. It met up with elements of the 5th Cavalry on October 12, and it was agreed that 5th Cavalry would take precedence on the road.

The 7th Cavalry Regiment, on the US 1st Cavalry Division's left flank, faced a tough assignment in attempting to cross the Yesong River—without bridging troops and equipment, and in the face of enemy opposition. It managed to secure a still-standing road and rail bridge over the river, but its fragile state could only support infantry movement. Having bombarded the KPA positions on the west bank of the river, the 7th managed to push its lead elements across on October 9. Despite KPA small-arms and mortar fire, the rest of the regiment managed to cross, and it pushed northward to Hanp'o-ri.

KPA forces were now compressed into what became known as the Kumch'on Pocket (named for the town). With the 7th Cavalry Regiment blocking any KPA exit from Kumch'on, the US 8th and 5th Cavalry regiments applied pressure on it from the south and the east. Supported by UNCOM air strikes, the stiff KPA resistance in the pocket was finally overcome by October 14. Considerable numbers of KPA troops managed to avoid capture, and retreated into the hills northeast of the town.

Dismayed by the collapse of his forces, Premier Kim Il-Sung, issued the following order: "Do not retreat one step further. Now we have no space in which to fall back." He also warned that anyone who deserted would be subject to being immediately shot, no matter what rank.

By the end of October 14, US I Corps troops had pushed through the key KPA positions located between the 38th Parallel and Pyongyang. The KPA front had to all intents and purposes collapsed and its forces were broken with command and control virtually non-existent. US President Truman met General MacArthur on Wake Island on October 15 to discuss "the final phase of UN action in Korea," as Truman called it. Given events in the DPRK, outright victory seemed in sight for UNCOM. Truman asked MacArthur if he thought a Chinese intervention threat was credible; MacArthur stated that he did not believe so. American intelligence agencies also held the same beliefs as MacArthur. Truman approved MacArthur's continued drive with an ultimate objective of demolishing the DPRK military and unifying the country under ROK President Syngman Rhee. Conferees accepted the idea that all resistance in DPRK would cease by Thanksgiving. Truman, now confident about the Korean War's outcome, queried MacArthur about releasing a division for redeployment to Europe.

Before going to Wake Island, MacArthur's chief of intelligence, Major-General Charles Willoughby, thought that the Soviets would achieve no immediate military advantage by confronting the United States at this point in time. He was aware that Beijing had deployed nine field armies (with 38 divisions) along the Manchurian border, but his view was that they had

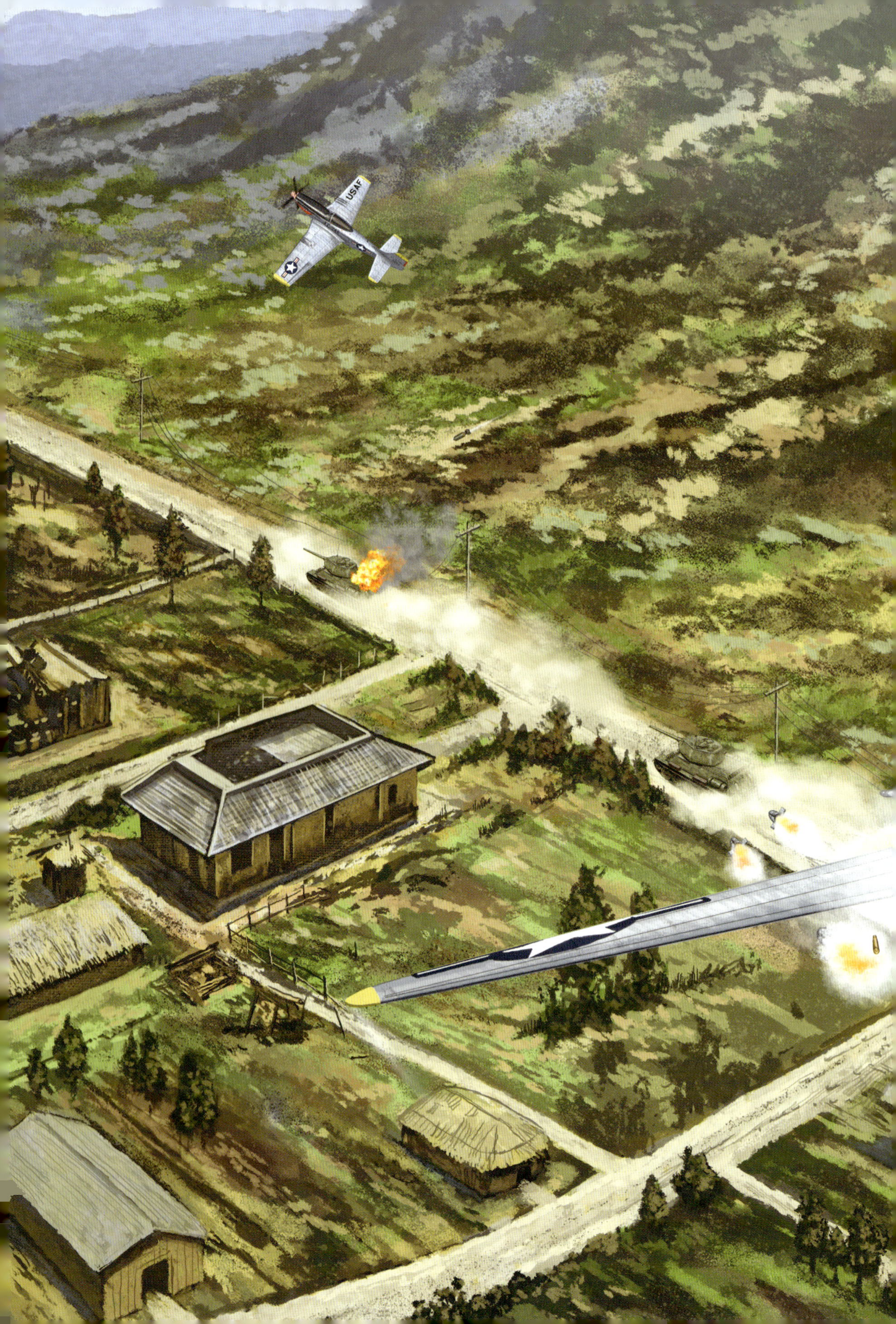
USAF

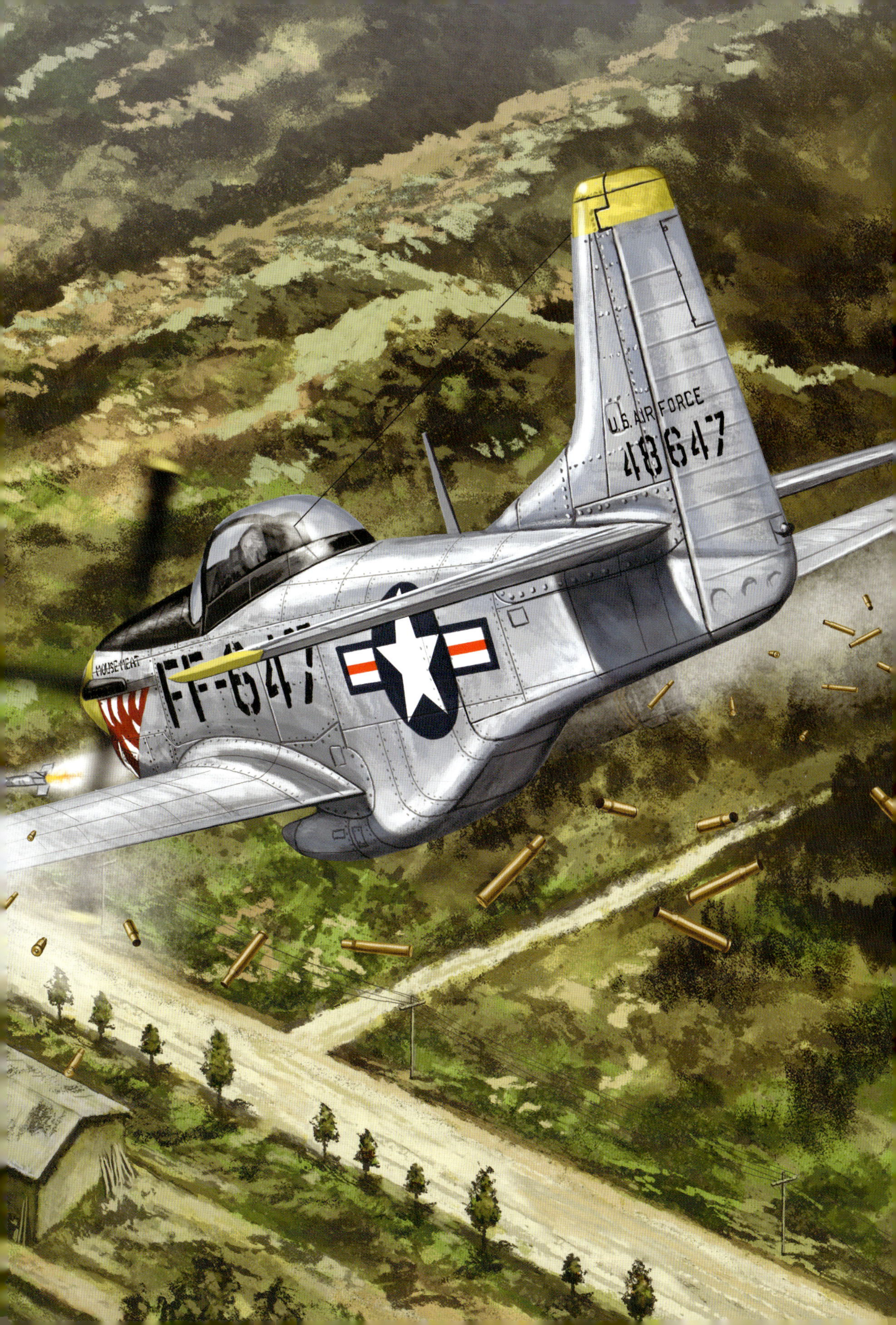
U.S. AIR FORCE
48647
FF-647
MOUSE MEAT

F-51 STRIKES, OCTOBER 1950 (PP. 28–29)

As UNCOM forces mobilized against the KPA, airpower provided a valuable asset. Much of the DPRK's air force had been destroyed by UNCOM planes in the Air Battle of South Korea between June 25 and July 20, 1950. The month-long battle for control of the air space over the peninsula ended in a UNCOM victory and the virtual destruction of the fledgling DPRK Air Force. In the wake of this victory UNCOM's air assets were able to concentrate their efforts on striking KPA ground forces, inflicting significant casualties, and bombing missions against the DPRK ports. Despite their obsolescent status, UNCOM's propeller-engined bombers and fighters and early jet fighter models could fly over Korean airspace virtually unopposed. To boot, the Fifth Air Force, much like the rest of the United States Air Force, was suffering from a lack of funds and resources, and used many World War II-era airframes. One such aircraft, which proved very effective in the close air support role, was the F-51D Mustang (**1**). Alongside its six .50-cal. Browning machine guns, the F-51D could deliver up to 1,000lb of bombs from two hardpoints, and 6–10 5in. T64 High Velocity Aircraft Rockets (**2**).

These two F-51Ds from the 18th Fighter Bomber Group's 12th Fighter Bomber Squadron are attacking two KPA T-34 tanks (**3**) moving along a road as they retreat from the ROK into the DPRK. Given the air superiority that UNCOM aviation assets enjoyed, these F-51Ds can confidently target these armored vehicles without significant fear of being shot down. UNCOM air superiority also meant that UNCOM ground forces could move freely during hours of daylight, whilst KPA units had to confine themselves to night attacks to avoid UNCOM air forces. Things would change when the USSR provided the DPRK and the PRC with its latest MiG-15 fighters, trained Korean and Chinese pilots to fly them, and committed the Soviet 64th Fighter Aviation Corps to support operations.

missed the critical period to intervene, since EUSAK already appeared to have the KPA on the run. Willoughby reasoned that if Moscow and Beijing were serious about the DPRK's long-term future, they would have rebuilt the KPA. China's warning about intervention was nothing more than "political blackmail" to save Kim Il-Sung. UNCOM's leadership could find reassurance in the fact that the US 1st Cavalry Division had already passed the 38th Parallel, and no intervention had followed.

X CORPS' LANDINGS AT WONSAN AND IWON, OCTOBER 17–29

MacArthur's plan was for Major-General Almond's X Corps to land on the Korean peninsula's east coast and move in parallel to the EUSAK northward. Wonsan was the largest DPRK east coast port, and the city also contained an airfield that could support UNCOM air operations. However, well before X Corps' landing, the ROK 3rd Division had breeched the border and was headed toward Wonsan. The ROK units pushed aside the KPA 5th Division elements, about 2,400 soldiers, and reached Wonsan's outskirts by October 10. The KPA's 24th Mechanized Artillery Brigade and some naval amphibious troops from the 945th Regiment defended the city. After an artillery exchange and street fighting, the city fell to the South Koreans the following day. The 1st Marine Air Wing's VMF-312, VMF (N)-513, and ground support units started landing at Wonsan's airfield on October 14, guaranteeing the US Marines their own close air support.

UNCOM's engineers not only had to repair damaged bridges, but also had to improve structures that could not withstand the weight of armored vehicles such as this M4A3 Sherman. (US Army)

The ships bearing the main body of the X Corps attack force—the US 1st Marine Division—departed Inch'on on the east coast on October 17. They headed into the Yellow Sea, and around the southern tip of the Korean peninsula, making for Wonsan. The sailing totaled around 830 miles. Having arrived off Wonsan, the ships remained offshore between October 19 and 25. The reason for this delay was that the ports of Wonsan and Hungnam had been heavily mined by the North Koreans. This posed a great risk to any troop-laden transports arriving in these ports, and a major UN naval effort was launched to remove this threat. The 21-ship Advance Force JTF 7 cleared Wonsan port of mines (starting October 10), delaying X Corps' landing. Four vessels were lost in the process. The seizure of Wonsan and the surrounding area by ROK I Corps helped speed up the mine-clearance process. Hungnam was cleared soon after. X Corps began to land early in the morning of October 26, with all combat elements ashore two days later.

The US 7th Division had begun loading its vehicles and equipment at Pusan in the southeast of the peninsula on October 14, and its infantry on the 16th. The planning and loading of supplies placed a considerable strain on Japan Logistical Command, and was a massive undertaking in itself. The

US 7th Division was heading for the port of Iwon in the DPRK, 150 miles northeast of Wonsan. In contrast to Wonsan, there were no mines found at Iwon. The 7th Division's mission was to advance inland toward the DPRK's northern border. The ROK Capital Division had already reached Iwon and secured the town several days prior to the start of the 7th's (unopposed) landing on the morning of October 29. Most of its elements were ashore by November 9.

Part of X Corps' role was to seize industrial areas, dams, and hydroelectric plants. The DPRK exported significant quantities of coal and electricity to Manchuria and the PRC, and control of these would put pressure on the Chinese economy.

The ROK Capital Division continued to push north toward the Chosin (Changjin) Reservoir. KPA resistance had faltered and the ROK I and II corps appeared likely to reach the Yalu River, which marked the border between the DPRK and the PRC. UNCOM's forces had achieved a spectacular result. Only a few weeks earlier, the KPA had bottled up MacArthur's forces at Pusan. Now, UNCOM was on the verge of defeating the KPA.

THE FALL OF PYONGYANG, OCTOBER 15–20

Due to the problems associated with moving food, fuel and ammunition north of the Han River, IX Corps had remained south of the river, leaving the advance northward to I Corps. Walker now planned to bring IX Corps forward to assist with the drive into the DPRK and on to the Chinese border at the Yalu River: the ROK III Corps would take over IX Corps' present responsibilities. To assist with logistical supply, the 3rd Logistical Command was assigned to EUSAK from Inch'on. Reconstruction of the damaged rail

Troops from the 5th Cavalry Regiment, 1st Cavalry Division fire on KPA troops from a railroad station during the fighting for Pyongyang. (US Army)

infrastructure became a priority, particularly the damaged and destroyed railroad bridges over the main rivers, as well as road bridges.

Changes in the weather also made the next stages of EUSAK's advance difficult, as torrential rains turned many routes into mud. On October 16, EUSAK's 7th Cavalry Regiment took the town of Namch'onjom, followed soon after by Sohung.

General Paik Sun Yup's ROK 1st Division was also making good progress on the right flank of the US 1st Cavalry Division. It fought a heavy battle with a KPA regimental force near Miudong, northeast of Namch'onjom, on October 15.

General Walker was eager for the advance to gain momentum (road congestion was one factor slowing it down), and ordered the US 24th Infantry Division to take the city of Sariwon from the south before driving on Pyongyang. The 27th British Commonwealth Brigade was also ordered to attack the city, if it was not needed to support the 7th Cavalry Regiment. At this point, all EUSAK major units were vying for the honor of being the first to enter the DPRK capital. The terrain between Sariwon and Pyongyang (only 35 miles apart) was mostly flat and conducive to a rapid advance. The heights before Sariwon were expected to make a good defensive position for the KPA, impeding any further UNCOM advance on Pyongyang. Yet the city fell with minimal resistance, with Commonwealth units entering the badly damaged town on October 17. That night, confusing episodes occurred with EUSAK troops believing KPA soldiers arriving in the town from the south to be ROK troops, and the North Koreans thinking the EUSAK soldiers were Soviet troops. Close-quarter fighting broke out when both sides realized the truth of the matter.

The road to Pyongyang now lay open. The US I Corps was fast approaching the capital from the south, and the ROK forces were beginning to envelop the city from the east, threatening to cut the routes out to the north.

One of the largest artillery pieces available to UNCOM units was the 155mm howitzer. This indirect fire support weapon could launch a projectile more than 8 miles and offered a sustained rate of fire of 40 rounds per hour. (US Army)

ADVANCE TO PYONGYANG, OCTOBER 15–19, 1950

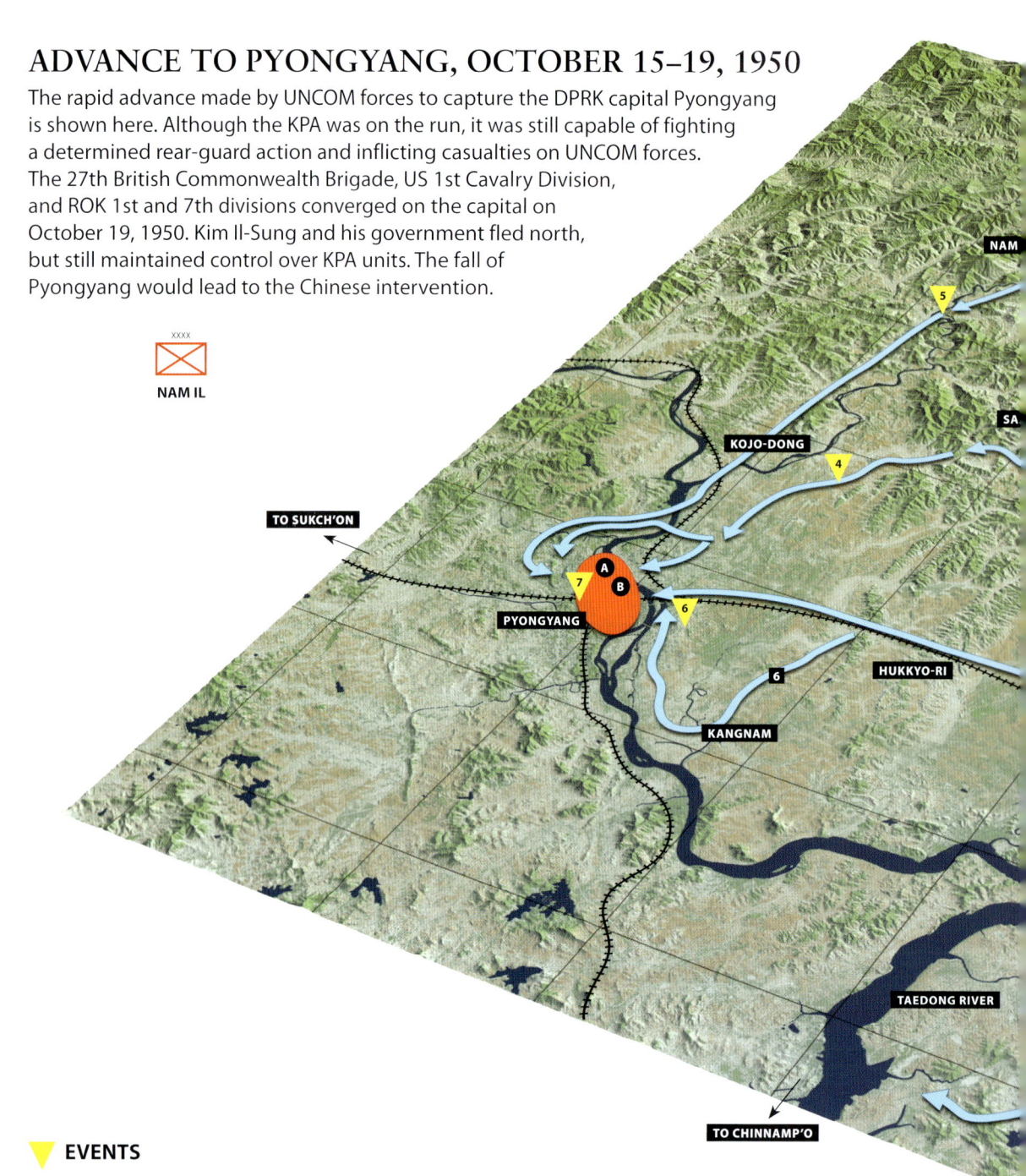

The rapid advance made by UNCOM forces to capture the DPRK capital Pyongyang is shown here. Although the KPA was on the run, it was still capable of fighting a determined rear-guard action and inflicting casualties on UNCOM forces. The 27th British Commonwealth Brigade, US 1st Cavalry Division, and ROK 1st and 7th divisions converged on the capital on October 19, 1950. Kim Il-Sung and his government fled north, but still maintained control over KPA units. The fall of Pyongyang would lead to the Chinese intervention.

EVENTS

1. October 17–19: Elements of the US 24th Infantry Division move north through Anak toward Chinnamp'o, where the Taedong River enters the Yellow Sea. The 19th Infantry Regiment secures ferry points on the southern Taedong River, which will allow UN forces to cross the river to Chinnamp'o.

2. October 17–19: The 27th British Commonwealth Brigade moves north from Hungsu-ri in support of UNCOM's assault on Pyongyang.

3. October 17–19: The 7th Regiment, US 1st Cavalry Division, moves north through the mountains from Sohung in an effort to bypass major roads clogged with tanks, vehicles, and refugees. It joins the main highway from the south to the North Korean capital at Hwangju. Many KPA units surrender to the advancing UNCOM forces due to a lack of food, ammunition, and fuel.

4. October 18: Elements of the ROK 1st Division, driving on Pyongyang from the southeast against light opposition, enter the city outskirts. Almost the entire division is inside the city before nightfall.

5. October 18–19: The ROK II Corps' 7th Division switches from the central axis of advance in the DPRK to support Pyongyang's capture. By late afternoon on October 18, the division's 8th Regiment moves into the northern part of Pyongyang and occupies Kim Il-Sung University.

6. October 19: Advance elements of the reinforced US 5th Cavalry Regiment and the 3rd Battalion, Royal Australian Regiment enter the outskirts of Pyongyang. Assisted by Fifth Air Force close air support, UNCOM forces destroy North Korean tanks blocking their path to the capital. Pyongyang's main industrial and government seat liesin the north of the city. US 1st Cavalry Division troops have to capture a highway and railroad bridge spanning the Taedong, which KPA sappers subsequently destroy.

7. Remnants from the KPA's 17th and 32nd divisions, estimated to be about 8,000 soldiers, attempt to hold back the ROK 1st Division, but soon yield. Their efforts have allowed some KPA units to retreat to the Chongch'on River.

Note: gridlines are shown at intervals of 20km (12.43 miles)

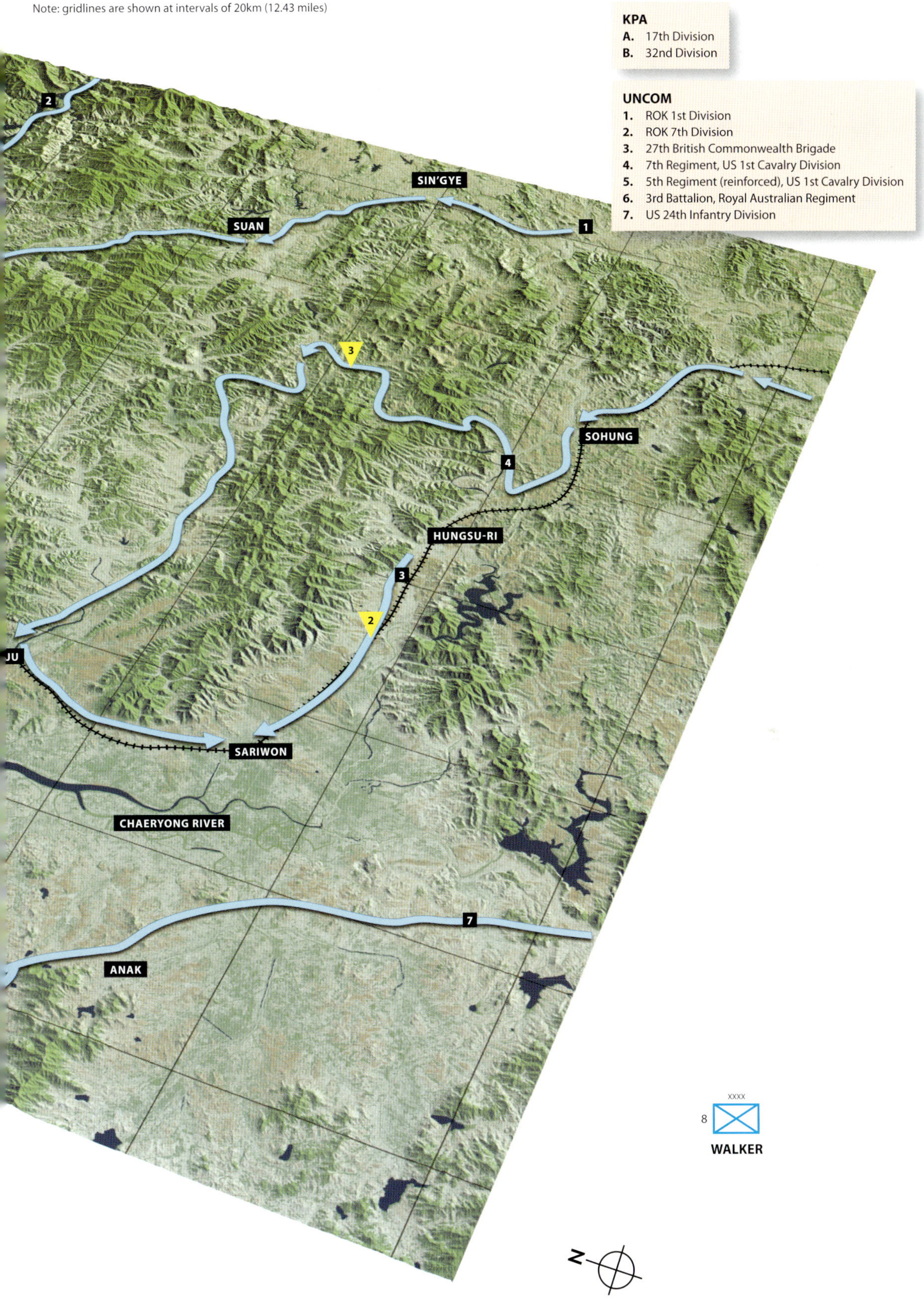

X Corps' original flanking maneuver after landing on the east coast at Wonsan had already been executed by ROK Army units under Eighth Army control before any landing had taken place. On October 17, the ROK 6th, 7th and 8th divisions from ROK II Corps began racing northwest across the peninsula, seeking to be first to enter Pyongyang, ahead of EUSAK on the east coast. The writing was on the wall for the KPA 17th and 32nd divisions' troops defending the capital. Most of these, it was expected, would withdraw northward across the Chongch'on River. Having secured the main road and rail bridges leading into the city, US 1st Division troops entered Pyongyang on October 19, followed soon after by the ROK 1st Division. Most KPA soldiers in the city were too demoralized to fight and were quick to surrender. A special UNCOM task force named Indianhead entering the North Korean capital to secure key government buildings and installations, and gather intelligence, all of which was turned over to MacArthur's headquarters.

On October 20 General MacArthur flew in from Tokyo to meet briefly with generals Walker and Stratemeyer. The US 7th Cavalry Regiment marched southwest by night on October 22 to secure the port city of Chinnamp'o. Meanwhile, Walker had established his EUSAK headquarters in Pyongyang in a building that had previously housed Kim Il-Sung's headquarters.

REACHING THE YALU, OCTOBER 20–23

On October 20, the US 187th Airborne RCT performed a mission to parachute behind enemy lines at two sites between the towns of Sukch'on and Sunch'on, about 30 miles north of Pyongyang. This maneuver sought to trap DPRK officials and troops fleeing north from the capital. MacArthur had approved the action on October 16. The US Fifth Air Force prepared the landing site by strafing the drop zone using fighter aircraft. The 1st and 3rd battalions of the 187th Airborne RCT dropped into the first zone near Sukch'on airlifted by C-119s and C-47s. They seized the hills dominating Sukch'on, cleared the town itself, and established road and rail blocks on key routes leading into it. The 2nd Battalion of the US 187th Airborne RCT landed in the second zone near Sunch'on, against little resistance. A link-up soon took place in the town with elements of the ROK 6th Division, which had pushed up from the southeast. Hundreds of tons of equipment, weapons, vehicles, and supplies had also been airlifted in together with the paratroopers. MacArthur was present to watch the airdrop take place, and was apparently so impressed that he commented to reporters shortly afterwards that the war would be shortly "coming to an end." However, the 187th RCT's actions failed to cut off any KPA units, as they had already retreated north beyond the two towns and were moving across the Chongch'on River.

Major-General Milburn had ordered the US I Corps to continue the advance beyond Pyongyang within hours of its fall. The objective was to reach the "MacArthur Line" roughly 35 miles to the south of the border with China on the Yalu River. The US 24th Infantry Division and the 27th British Commonwealth Brigade, supported by a battalion each of armor and artillery, headed the move north, whilst the ROK 1st, 6th and 8th divisions played a supporting role. The unfortunate KPA 239th Regiment was virtually annihilated at Yongyu, caught between the advancing UNCOM units from the south, and the 3rd Battalion of the 187th RCT from the north. The 27th

The 187th Airborne RCT dropped north of Pyongyang on October 20, 1950 in an attempt to trap fleeing DPRK officials and KPA units. The effort was partially successful. Fifth Air Force had to use every available C-119 to execute this mission. (US Army)

British Commonwealth Brigade then continued north to relieve the 187th RCT from its Sukch'on positions.

Task Force Rodgers—a combined infantry–armor force based around 1st Battalion, 8th Cavalry Regiment and a company from 70th Tank Battalion, under the command of Lieutenant-Colonel William Rodgers—now moved north from Pyongyang to link up with the 187th RCT troops at Sunch'on.

Premier Kim Il-Sung initially established his new base in Sinuiju, on the banks of the Yalu and next to the Chinese border in the northeast of the DPRK, but soon this transferred 150 miles northwest to Kanggye in the mountainous DPRK interior. Kanggye provided good access to further paths of retreat north, into China, and lay on routes into both northeast and northwest Korea. Evidence was now emerging further south of war crimes committed by KPA troops, with numerous unarmed American prisoners being shot by the retreating North Korean troops.

UNCOM's drive north continued. On October 22, Task Force Elephant (based around C Company, 6th Medium Tank Battalion), with ROK 1st Division in tow, headed out of Pyongyang through Sunch'on, and on to Kunu-ri. The following day, Paik's ROK 1st Division headed down the valley of the Chongch'on River towards Anju. Following repairs to damaged bridges, Paik's division crossed the Chongch'on, and then attacked north toward Unsan. The 27th British Commonwealth Brigade reached Sinanju on October 23, and the following day began crossing the Chongch'on. The 24th Infantry Division meanwhile had reached Sunan, 12 miles north of Pyongyang.

The ROK 6th Division headed upriver on the Chongch'on aiming for Ch'osan on the Yalu River, pushing the UNCOM advance to its furthest limits. To the east, the ROK 8th Division pushed into the mountains, reaching Tokch'on late on October 23. Other ROK reconnaissance units came within five miles of the border near Ch'osan. One unit reported that KPA forces had retreated across the Yalu into Manchuria.

Concerns were raised over the length of UNCOM's growing logistical lines (which now stretched back to Inch'on), the lack of transportation, the poor state of the DPRK's roads, and the time and resources needed to restore broken bridges. The US Fifth Air Force had to transport supplies to airfields from Japan to Korea for further ground distribution or to be parachuted into the field. There was a possible risk of moving north too quickly, risking units being cut off and destroyed.

Since victory appeared at hand, Walker requested that bulk ammunition shipments arriving from the United States to Korea be diverted to Japan. Some ammunition supply ships even returned to San Francisco for unloading since the cargo appeared to be unnecessary. In addition, MacArthur now identified the 2nd Infantry Division (part of IX Corps) for transfer to Europe. Some US 1st Cavalry Division elements also started to turn in their equipment. Units from other UN nations were now arriving in Korea, including the Turkish Brigade. However, the Chinese reaction to events would prove that the war was far from over.

THE CHINESE FIRST PHASE OFFENSIVE, OCTOBER 19–NOVEMBER 5

Marshal Peng Dehuai's Fourth Field Army's troops had begun crossing into the DPRK from Manchuria from October 13 onward. Because they crossed mountainous terrain, often at night, UN intelligence assets failed to detect the movements of these units. They took up positions about 50 miles south of the Yalu River, concealed in the mountainous terrain and overwatching the transit routes through the valleys. On October 19, the PVA formally crossed the Yalu River under strict secrecy. Around 250,000,000 Chinese soldiers poured into the highland area above the Chongch'on River, the last major water obstacle in the western DPRK before the Chinese border.

The Chinese plan for its First Phase Offensive was to drive south, then west to cut off the EUSAK from the Chongch'on River. Supporting the 40th

The PVA was able to cross into the DPRK by marching across the Yalu River in October 1950. UNCOM's Fifth Air Force was unable to destroy all the bridges across the river, but this later became a moot point after freezing temperatures froze the river solid. (Department of Defense)

Army was the 39th Army on its right. The latter's mission was to strike the pinned-down US 1st Cavalry and ROK 1st divisions. On the 40th Army's left was the 38th Army, whose units would move in parallel with the 40th Army to hit the EUSAK's flanks and attempt to collapse it.

On October 19 MacArthur had issued Operations Order No. 4, which lifted the restriction on any UN units other than the ROK operating north of a line from Chongju through Kunu-ri and Yongwon to Hamhung on the peninsula's east coast. UNCOM commanders were now free to press forward to the northern limits of Korea. Some JCS officers objected and believed MacArthur had overstepped his authority. MacArthur countered that Secretary of Defense George Marshall's letter allowed him wide latitude strategically and tactically, authorizing him to modify the directive. His faith in UNCOM force superiority was unshakeable, and he trusted that airpower would isolate any large-scale Chinese movement into the DPRK.

The US 24th Infantry Division's 21st Infantry Regiment moved north to Sinuiju, which neighbored the Chinese city of Antung. Earlier in the war, two Fifth Air Force F-51Ds accidently strafed a PLAAF airfield near Antung, and a B-29 bombed a nearby railroad marshalling yard on September 22, both of which provoked angry reactions from Beijing. Opposing the 21st Infantry Regiment's drive was the depleted KPA 17th Armored Division. The remaining 24th Infantry Division regiments, the 5th and 19th, moved north to Kusong, and approached within 25 miles south of the Yalu River.

The first clash between UNCOM forces and PVA troops took place eight miles west of Onjong. On October 25, the ROK 3rd Battalion from 2nd Regiment, 6th Division encountered Chinese soldiers at a roadblock, thinking they were KPA troops. The ROK battalion was hit hard by the Chinese, and massive casualties were inflicted with just about half of the battalion managing to escape. The ROK regiment's 2nd Battalion tried to help its sister unit, but was forced back. Walker's staff interrogated a PVA prisoner who disclosed that his unit had occupied the hills near Pukchin since October 17. China was clearly now in the war.

The ROK II Corps appeared near to collapse on the right flank of EUSAK's I Corps. To bolster this flank, Walker detached the ROK 7th Division from the EUSAK's I Corps to the ROK II Corps on October 29. The ROK 7th Division would hold a defensive line north of Won-ni on the Chongch'on River. The ROK II Corps' 8th Division moved north and extended the 7th Division's defensive line and filled a gap with the ROK 1st Division. Walker further ordered the US 1st Cavalry Division, occupying Pyongyang, to move forward. The cavalrymen positioned themselves north of the ROK 1st Division in Unsan. Like the ROK 6th Division, the 1st Division's 15th Regiment, which had occupied Unsan, also encountered Chinese forces in hills above the city. The PVA's 38th and 40th armies did not stop at Onjong or Unsan, but pushed the ROK II Corps further south.

Although UNCOM forces had clashed with Chinese forces and captured some prisoners, MacArthur's staff maintained that the presence of a few volunteer Chinese units would not make a difference overall, and moreover Walker had realigned his units to compensate. The 8th Cavalry Regiment had pushed beyond Unsan. Still, if major Chinese forces had entered the war, it would require a shift to the defensive, and EUSAK and X Corps planners had to plug any gaps between their forces to ward off any probing Chinese attacks that might expose vulnerabilities in UNCOM's front. There was still scant evidence of the scale and scope of China's intervention. With the exception of the information provided by some Chinese prisoners, most UN intelligence sources had focused on target development for air bombardment against the DPRK.

The Chinese 39th Army prepared to hit the ROK 15th Regiment, 1st Division east of Unsan. The city had some distinct advantages to any attacking force coming from the north. Above Unsan were hills that masked and disguised Chinese movements. In addition, the city was bordered on the west, south, and east by the Samt'an River, which could delay any retreat or reinforcement to the US 8th Cavalry Regiment's three battalions. If the Chinese captured the bridges over the river, they might isolate the 8th Cavalry and the ROK 15th Regiment. The 8th Cavalry faced at best a severe mauling, at worst destruction.

The Chinese hit the ROK 15th Regiment first on November 1, scattering the regiment's three battalions. Soon, the ROK units were falling back and exposing the 1st Battalion, 8th Cavalry Regiment to PVA probes. If the PVA drove out the 15th Regiment, then they could isolate the 8th Cavalry. Walker believed the ROK II Corps had ceased to provide any meaningful combat capabilities. If the ROK II Corps failed, then the next defensible position was at the Chongch'on River at Kunu-ri where UNCOM engineers had constructed a pontoon bridge. The 1st Cavalry Division was now exposed. I Corps' G-2 (Intelligence) reported to MacArthur's staff that the Chinese intended to conduct major combat operations against UNCOM. MacArthur's staff still disagreed.

Two 8th Cavalry battalions, the 2nd on the left and 1st on the right, defended Unsan from ridges above the city. The PVA's 115th and 116th divisions infiltrated the positions on each battalion's flank. The 116th Division bore the brunt of the fighting against the 8th Cavalry Regiment. The Chinese employed stealth, deception, and night attacks to exploit weak spots throughout the UNCOM defensive lines. At 1930hrs on November 1, the PVA struck the two battalions, launching "human wave" attacks and blowing their bugles to announce each attack on the Americans. Facing potential encirclement, the US 1st Cavalry Division's commander ordered the 8th Cavalry Regiment out of Unsan south at around midnight. Fighting died down at 0130hrs on November 2, and the three cavalry battalions moved toward Ipsok. The PVA anticipated this withdrawal and constructed roadblocks at key exit points. Nonetheless, the 1st and 2nd battalions escaped. Not so the 3rd Battalion. Heavy engagements with the Chinese forced the 3rd Battalion to defend a position with three tanks. The 5th and 7th Cavalry regiments attempted to relieve the beleaguered battalion, but their efforts failed, and it was lost.

The overall strategic situation had evolved. With a possible full-scale Chinese intervention, was this to be considered the start of a global or limited conflict? If the war was "limited," then UNCOM's conventional forces would have to fight with existing capabilities. Washington would have to cancel any divisional redeployment plans from Korea to Europe: sending the US 2nd Infantry Division to Europe was now impossible. Marshall had to expedite requests for 40,000 replacements from the United States to Korea. Other nations that had decided not to send military units to UNCOM had to re-evaluate their decisions. Some American, UN, and ROK troops, within the EUSAK, had already fallen back to defensive positions near the Chongch'on River.

Front line, October 26–November 24, 1950

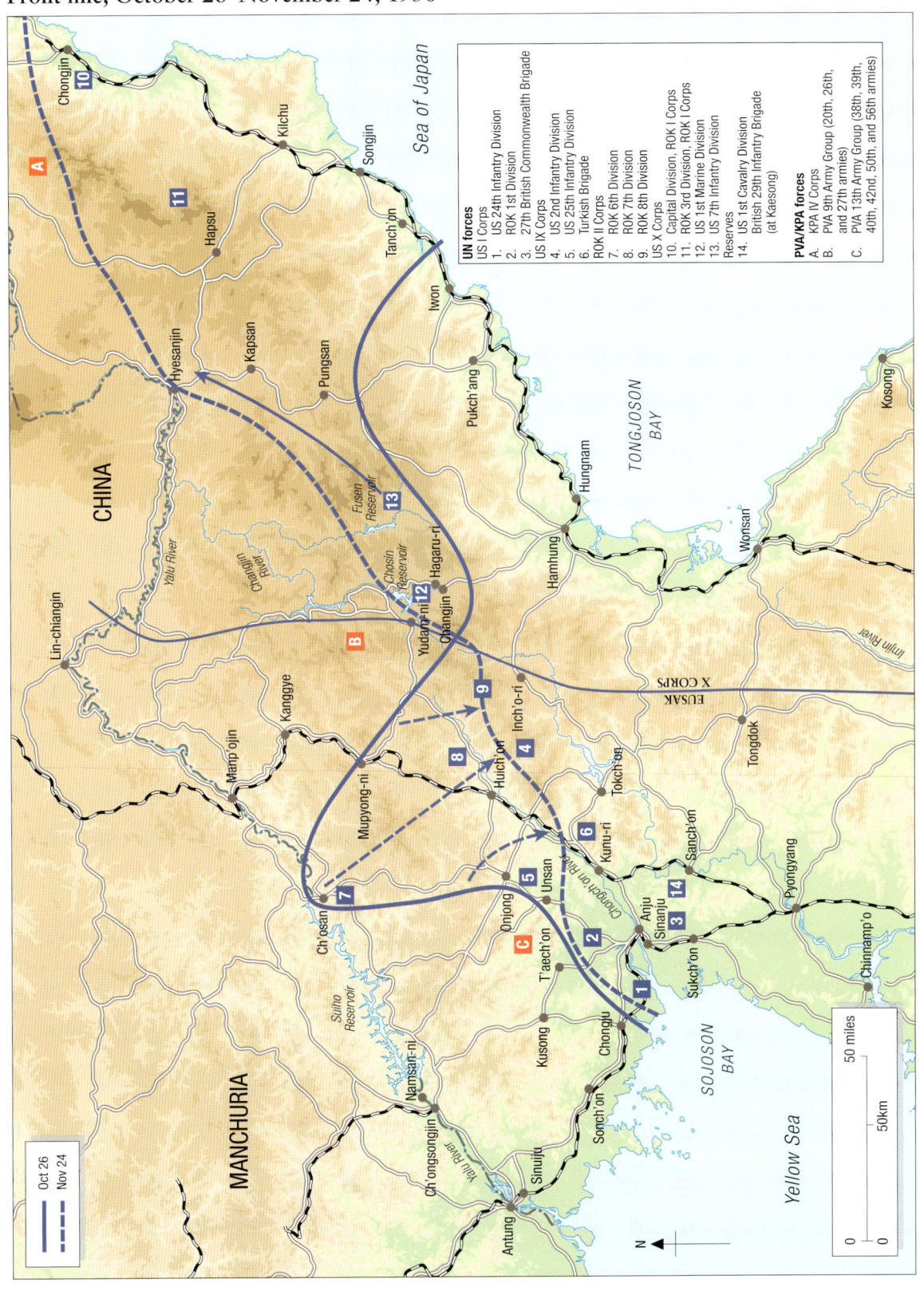

UN forces

US I Corps
1. US 24th Infantry Division
2. ROK 1st Division
3. 27th British Commonwealth Brigade

US IX Corps
4. US 2nd Infantry Division
5. US 25th Infantry Division
6. Turkish Brigade

ROK II Corps
7. ROK 6th Division
8. ROK 7th Division
9. ROK 8th Division

US X Corps
10. Capital Division, ROK I Corps
11. ROK 3rd Division, ROK I Corps
12. US 1st Marine Division
13. US 7th Infantry Division

Reserves
14. US 1st Cavalry Division
British 29th Infantry Brigade (at Kaesong)

PVA/KPA forces

A. KPA IV Corps
B. PVA 9th Army Group (20th, 26th, and 27th armies)
C. PVA 13th Army Group (38th, 39th, 40th, 42nd, 50th, and 56th armies)

MacArthur's airpower also faced challenges. He had authorized two weeks of concerted air attacks against the DPRK starting on November 5. Fifth Air Force attacked the new KPA/PVA Combined Headquarters at Kanggye, supply points, suspected arsenals, and troop concentration centers. MacArthur also ordered the bridges across the Yalu to be destroyed, but Washington restricted aircrews from bombing the Chinese side—a difficult task for aircrews flying high-altitude B-29 missions. The Seventh Fleet's TF 77 carrier aircraft supported strikes on the DPRK's east coast bridges. Not all the Yalu bridges were taken out. Chinese MIG-15 opposition harassed attacking UN aircraft. The bitter cold snap that would descend on the Korean peninsula from Siberia in mid-November 1950 would cause the Yalu to freeze over, allowing Chinese forces to cross by foot or vehicle.

The Chinese First Phase Offensive came to a halt on November 5. Peng's 38th Army had driven UN forces from the area around Unsan, and had brought relief to the embattled KPA. Their own asessment of the results was that overall it was satisfactory. Chinese forces now withdrew into the hills to regroup.

A reorganization of UNCOM forces took place in the west and center of the peninsula. On the left flank (the western area of responsibility) was US I Corps, consisting of the US 24th Infantry Division, ROK 1st Division, and 27th British Commonwealth Brigade. In the center was US IX Corps, composed of the 2nd and 25th Infantry divisions plus the 1st Turkish Armed Forces Command (aka the Turkish Brigade). The right flank was held by the ROK II Corps with the ROK 6th, 7th, and 8th divisions. A key logistics centre was created at Kunu-ri. During the recent fighting, some of UNCOM's units only had a day's supply of ammunition and gasoline.

THE EAST: US X CORPS PUSHES NORTH, OCTOBER 25–NOVEMBER 25

MacArthur's original concept to destroy the KPA had X Corps executing a pincer movement west to support EUSAK's capture of Pyongyang. However, with EUSAK's rapid advance to the capital, the movement forced MacArthur to change X Corps' objectives. X Corps was to head toward the Yalu River, through the mountainous terrain of northeast Korea.

The region had some notable characteristics. The Wonsan and Hungnam areas included the DPRK's major industrial capacity, whose outputs included processed chemicals, medical supplies, fertilizer, and other products. These two cities also contained the major regional population centers, about 170,000 civilians. With a relatively small civilian population, there was little concern about an uprising occurring in any rear areas. The high mountainous terrain shielded enemy movements and offered few transit routes. Winter was coming and temperatures were beginning to fall. The weather would play a key role in the fighting in this sector.

Following the landings, the ROK Capital Division (I Corps) attacked northward toward the Chinese border. It captured Songjin on October 28, over 100 miles northeast of Hungnam. By October 30, elements of the division had also reached the southern end of Fusen (Pujon) Reservoir. The ROK 3rd Division followed behind the Capital, aiming for Hapsu. The Capital Division then moved northeast up the coastal road toward the border with the USSR near Chongjin; any KPA opposition encountered was relatively ineffective, and the industrial city fell on November 25. Meanwhile, the ROK 3rd Division protected Wonsan, and the US 1st Marine Division had moved 30 miles northwest on its assigned axis of advance from Hamhung to the Chosin Reservoir by November 24.

The US 7th Infantry Division made the greatest gains. From its landing site at Iwon, it moved north and pushed aside any KPA opposition. The division's 31st Regimental Combat Team (RCT) encountered some 200 PVA soldiers on November 15 at the Pujon (Fusen) Reservoir, and overcame the limited opposition offered. The 7th Infantry Division then met up with the US 1st Marine Division. The 7th Infantry Division's 32nd RCT reached the Yalu River near Hyesanjin on November 21 and was at Sin'galp'ajin a week later. X Corps appeared well ahead of schedule. The US 1st Marine Division planned now to break out of the Chosin Reservoir, join up with the ROK II Corps, and split the DPRK in half.

THE CHINESE SECOND PHASE OFFENSIVE, NOVEMBER 25–DECEMBER 24

The Chinese Second Phase Offensive would witness two major battles: the battle of the Chongch'on River in the west of the peninsula, and the battle of Chosin Reservoir in the east. As UN forces resumed the offensive, confident that rapid victory would ensue, the PVA launched major, coordinated attacks that surprised UNCOM. The latter would switch rapidly to the defense, and by the end of the offensive in late December 1950, UNCOM would find itself ejected from the DPRK.

Battle of the Chongch'on River, November 25–December 2, 1950

The Chongch'on River valley was a major terrain feature in the DPRK. It held the principal roads and rail line for any advance to the DPRK–PRC border, and on to Kanggye. Beyond the Chongch'on Valley lay mountainous terrain guarded by the towns of T'aech'on, Unsan, and Onjong, with limited routes beyond them, making the area a natural defensive barrier against any incursion from the south. Control of this area would be heavily contested.

The only major KPA unit actively engaged on the Korean front was the IV Corps comprising one division and two brigades. This corps was opposite the ROK I Corps in the northeast of the DPRK. Of greater consquence were c. 300,000 Chinese troops massed in the mountains opposite the EUSAK and X Corps. Facing EUSAK's forces in the western sector was the Chinese 13th Army Group, comprising the 38th, 39th, 40th, 42nd, 50th, and 56th armies, totaling some 200,000 troops. The XIII Army Group had crossed the Yalu border into the DPRK in late October 1950 at Sinuiju and Manp'ojin, and had taken part in the First Phase Offensive in early November. In the center of the country were the Chinese 9th Army Group's 20th, 26th, and 27th armies. The 9th Army Group's consituent armies, which had entered North Korea across the Yalu at Manp'ojin and Lin-chiangin in early November, consisted of four divisions, not three, and totaled over 120,000 soldiers facing the US X Corps zone.

UNCOM's analysis of the Chinese presence at this point amounted to only a dozen or so Chinese divisions, based on two supposed defensive lines:

The Chongch'on Valley, November 25–28, 1950

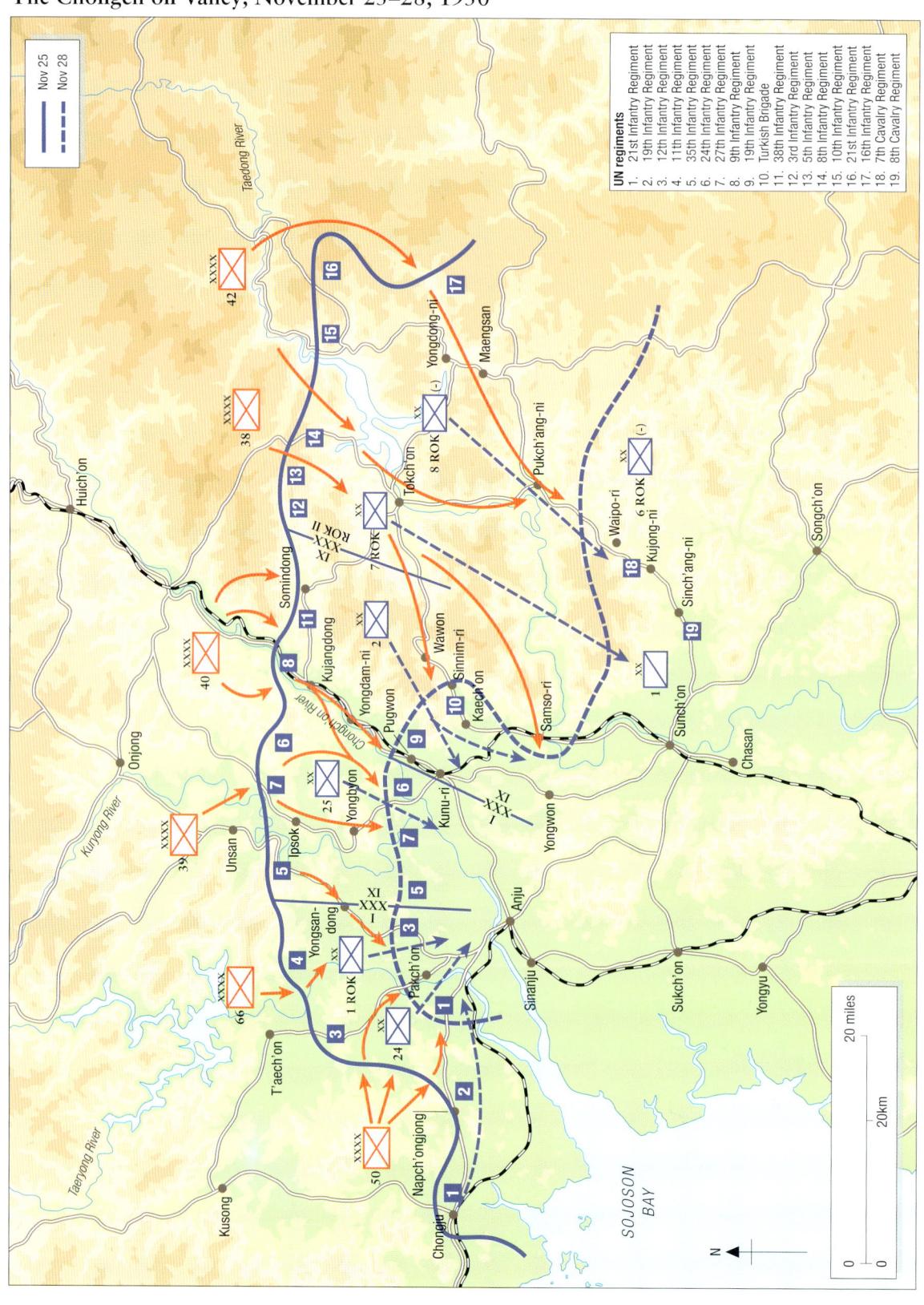

one stretching from Chongju northeast through T'aech'on and Unsan, and the other running northeast through Kusong, Onjong, and Huich'on and on to the Chosin Reservoir.

UNCOM's alignment of forces for the continuation of the push north, deep into the DPRK, was as follows. Walker's US I Corps secured the left flank, comprising the US 24th Infantry Division, the ROK 1st Division, and the 27th British Commonwealth Brigade. The US IX Corps held the center, comprising the US 25th Infantry Division, the US 2nd Infantry Division, and the Turkish Brigade. The ROK II Corps held positions on the right of the US IX Corps further east, comprising the ROK 6th, 7th, and 8th divisions. Walker held the US 1st Cavalry Division and the recently arrived British 29th Infantry Brigade as the EUSAK reserves. The 1st Cavalry Division were tasked with protecting the forward EUSAK supply points at Kunu-ri south of the Chongch'on River in the IX Corps sector, and those at Sukch'on adjacent to Route 1 in the I Corps sector. The British 29th Infantry Brigade was assembling at Kaesong, 30 miles north of Seoul. Walker could also rely on the unassigned 187th Airborne RCT, the Philippine 10th Battalion Combat Team, and the ROK III Corps. One Thai and one Dutch battalion would also soon be available to him.

EUSAK's move north began early on November 24, when the US 24th Infantry Division and the ROK 1st Division of Milburn's I Corps were sent west and northwest toward Chongju and T'aech'on; the 27th British Commonwealth Brigade remained in reserve. Coulter's IX Corps sent the US 2nd Infantry Division toward Huich'on, proceeding steadily, while the US 25th Infantry Division (Task Force Dolman) moved on Unsan and Onjong; the Turkish Brigade was held in reserve at Kunu-ri. Major-General Yu Jae Hung, commander of ROK II Corps, sent his 7th and 8th divisions north through the mountains, heading for the Yalu River.

As US I Corps units reached Chongju on November 25, they found it abandoned. The ROK 1st Division's progress toward T'aech'on encountered resistance during the night from counterattacking Chinese troops supported

Troops from the 3rd Battalion, Royal Australian Regiment hitch a ride on an M4A3E8 Sherman deep inside the DPRK in late November 1950. 3RAR was Australia's main land force contribution to the UN forces in the war, arriving in South Korea in late September 1950. The battalion was attached to 27th British Commonwealth Brigade. (Keystone/Getty Images)

A US 2nd Infantry Division machine-gun team overlooking the Chongch'on River valley. (US Army)

by artillery, forcing one of Paik's regiments back. The 1st Division was still several miles short of T'aech'on by nightfall on the 25th. Chinese fire and counterattacks had grown stronger on this second day of advance, but ground was still being covered by EUSAK and casualties had been light. Moreover, soon Almond's US X Corps would be attacking from the east. Now, however, was the moment the Chinese chose to strike in force. The Second Phase Offensive sought to contain the US I Corps in the west whilst pressurising EUSAK's center and enveloping its forces from the east via the ROK II Corps sector.

On the evening of November 25 the PVA's 39th and 40th armies from 13th Army Group launched a massive assault on the US 2nd Infantry Division's 15-mile front centered on the Chongch'on Valley, in IX Corps' sector. The US 9th Infantry Regiment on the division's left, holding the ridgelines west of the river with some elements across the river, was struck by a bi-regimental Chinese attack. The 38th Infantry Regiment, on the divisional right abutting the ROK II Corps sector, was attacked by a single PVA regiment. One Chinese regiment managed to infiltrate the gap between the US 9th and 38th Infantry regiments, overrunning a battalion command post and aid station in the rear.

Also in IX Corps' sector, to the west, the US 25th Infantry Division's Task Force Dolvin came under pressure during the night of November 25/26 from the Chinese 39th and 40th armies. The Chinese attacks forced a consolidation of Dolman's force and a battalion from the 24th Infantry Regiment into a new task force, Wilson. Other units began to organize a defense along the Chongch'on Valley on the 26th, tightening their positions and closing up gaps in between.

To the east, it was becoming clearer now that General Yu's ROK II Corps was struggling to hold the line, with Chinese pressure telling in the area around Yongdong-ni. Units from the PVA 38th and 42nd armies had also infiltrated between the ROK 7th and 8th divisions, pushing 10 miles south toward Tokch'on by the morning of November 26 and cutting the main corps supply route. The ROK II Corps front began to collapse by midday amid considerable confusion, with Yu's units withdrawing to the southwest. The Chinese 38th Army was now pushing west toward Sinnim-ri and Samso-ri, forcing the US 2nd Infantry Division in the east of IX Corps' sector back down the Chongch'on Valley to avoid being outflanked, first to Kujangdong, then to Yongdam-ni and Pugwon.

Chinese attacks from the 50th and 66th armies had struck west of the Chongch'on River in US I Corps' sector. The US 24th Infantry Division was held by the 50th Army, while the 66th Army struck the ROK 1st Division south of T'aech'on, threatening to outflank the 24th to the left, along the Taeryong River. The 24th Infantry began to withdraw to prevent this. PVA attacks continued throughout the night of November 27/28, with the 39th and 66th armies pressing down between the Taeryong and Kuryong rivers heading for the village of Yongsan-dong, which would allow good road access to the Chongch'on river crossings north of Anju. Yongsan-dong was captured, pushing back the remaining ROK 1st Division regiments, and threatening a deep penetration of the EUSAK line in this sector.

EUSAK's advance to the Yalu was now ordered to halt on the 28th, to prevent any threat of encirclement from the east. However, it was still not accepted at EUSAK HQ that a major Chinese offensive, the Second Phase, was now under way; the PVA's activities were still considered to be an active defense employing opportunistic counterattack. Coulter's IX Corps was now given responsibility for the collapsed ROK II Corps sector, widening its area of responsibility. At the same time, to compensate, responsibility for the US 25th Infantry Division's area of operations was transferred to US I Corps. Walker acted to prevent any further Chinese incursions from the northeast into EUSAK's rear by shifting the reserve US 1st Cavalry Division from Kunu-ri and Sukch'on on November 27 to block a main, deep route of advance to the Chinese along the road east of Sunch'on. Simultaneously, Brigadier-General Tahsin Yazici's Turkish Brigade from IX Corps was sent

With PVA forces heading south and pressurizing UNCOM forces, the latter faced major supply problems. The Fifth Air Force used its C-119s and other transports to resupply UNCOM's units. (US Air Force)

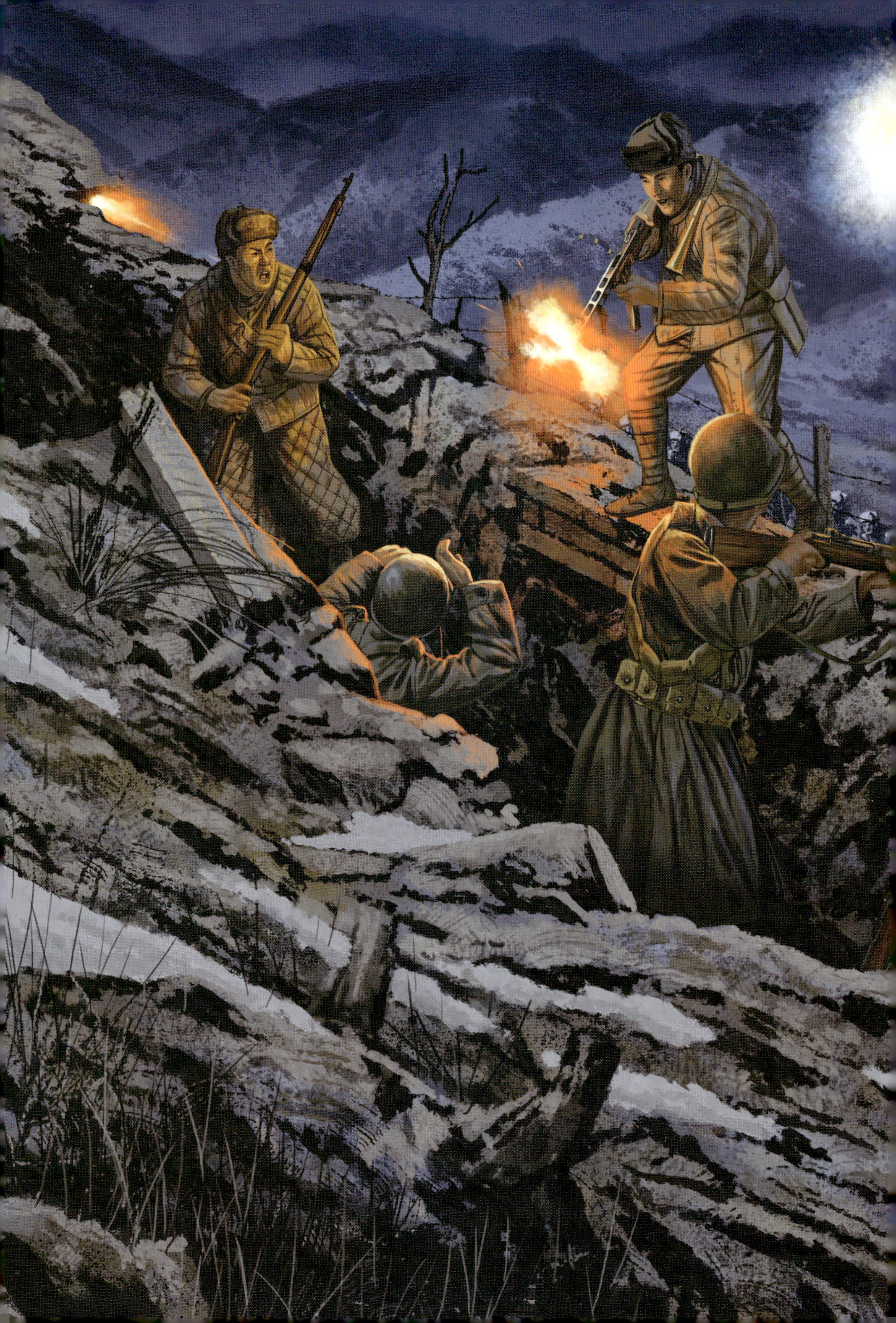

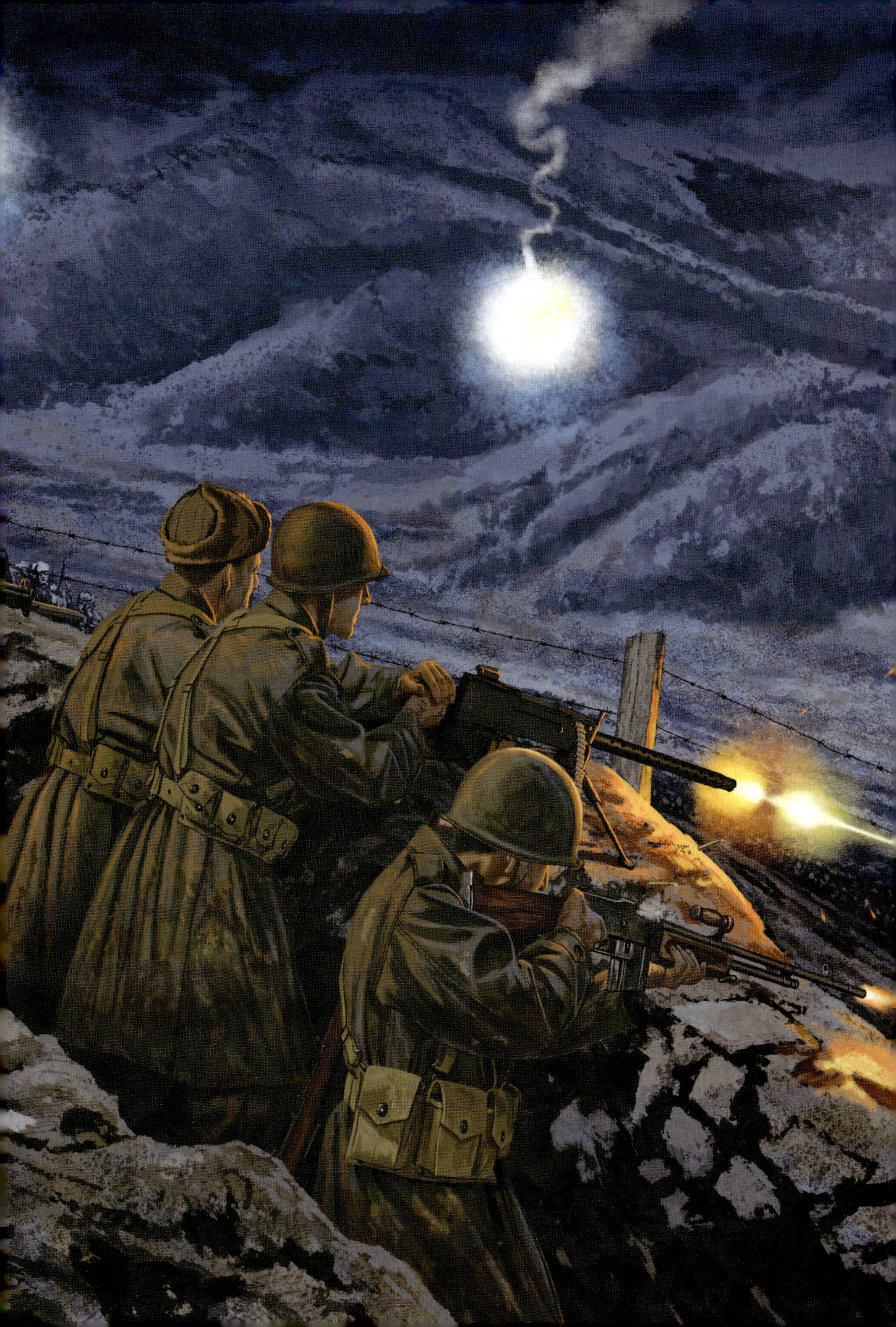

PVA NIGHT ATTACK IN THE CHONGCH'ON VALLEY, NOVEMBER 25, 1950 (PP. 48–49)

The advance north of Pyongyang proceeded well for UNCOM. As the EUSAK pushed the KPA out of the DPRK capital, Walker prepared his forces to defeat the remaining KPA units, which would allow him to move to the Yalu River, the border with China. The prevailing opinion among MacArthur's staff was that there was little chance of a major Chinese intervention in the DPRK. This was soon proved wrong.

On November 25, 1950, PVA forces struck the US 2nd Infantry Division at night along their forward positions. With bugles blaring and gongs sounding, the Chinese advanced against the US trenches in massed waves under the light of flares. Peng's forces suffered from a lack of adequate communications, which hampered command and control, planning, and attack execution. They overcame this by using bugles, drums, and flags to communicate between units. These acted as psychological weapons against UNCOM's forces, which not only warned of an impending attack, but also signaled another human wave assault. Chinese commanders were willing to accept large numbers of casualties.

The US infantrymen shown here are armed with a variety of weapons providing significant firepower, including (**1**) a Browning machine gun, (**2**) M1 rifles, and (**3**) a Browning Automatic Rifle. The weapons of their Chinese counterparts are not as advanced, and PVA units were sent into combat with a mixture of firearms. The Chinese soldiers who have reached the trench are armed with (**4**) a Soviet PPsH submachine gun, and (**5**) a World War II-era Japanese era Arisaka rifle.

east from Kunu-ri heading for positions east of Wawon; however, due to a misunderstanding, the brigade ended up on the Kunu-ri road 10 miles east of Kunu-ri. The 27th British Commonwealth Brigade from US I Corps moved north to replace the Turks at Kunu-ri.

In the US IX Corps' sector, pressure from attacks by the Chinese 38th and 40th armies continued against the US 2nd Infantry Division into the morning of the 28th. Walker now ordered the establishment of a defensive line stretching from Pakch'on in the east to Pugwon on the Chongch'on River, to which the US I and IX Corps would now withdraw, commencing in the afternoon of the 28th. The move was mostly completed by nightfall, although road congestion was a particular problem southward down the Chongch'on Valley, alongside attacks from the pursuing Chinese 40th Army. The ROK II Corps also withdrew from its positions to this new line during daylight on November 29.

The 27th British Commonwealth Brigade now moved to just south of Sunch'on, ready to support the US 2nd Infantry Division or the US 1st Cavalry Division as required. The Turkish Brigade, which had clashed with the Chinese 38th Army near Wawon and had retreated to Sinnim-ri, was now brought under control of the US 2nd Infantry Division, whose mission was to delay the Chinese as much as possible during the withdrawal.

It was becoming clear to Walker that a strong Chinese push was now aiming for Sunch'on (42nd Army, from the southwest) and Kunu-ri (38th Army, from the west). This threatened to cut off EUSAK to the rear from the east. The US 24th Infantry Division was now pulled back to Sunch'on, and assigned to IX Corps control from I Corps. The British 29th Infantry Brigade was attached to I Corps to compensate and moved north to Anju. Walker took the decision on November 29 to withdraw EUSAK further south to a line stretching from Sukch'on in the west, through Sunch'on, and on to Songch'on, to avoid envelopment.

The Chinese 40th Army attacked EUSAK's positions in the Kunu-ri sector on November 29. The Turkish Brigade was struck by attacks from the Chinese 38th Army at Sinnim-ri, forcing the brigade back to Kaech'on, where it took up positions on a small hill to the east of the town and inside the town itself. In I Corps' sector, west of the Chongch'on River, fewer Chinese attacks were launched. I Corps managed to withdraw its units south of the Chongch'on by November 30, avoiding the threat of being cut off by Chinese 40th Army forces heading down the Chongch'on Valley road to the east of the river. The bridges over the river at Anju were then blown.

Kunu-ri was ordered abandoned on November 29, with the Turkish Brigade withdrawing in some disorder, strung out along the road, and the US 2nd Infantry Division pulling south soon after under harassment of Chinese attacks. The roads south were clogged with fleeing civilians and this slowed

Turkish troops search Chinese prisoners shortly after their capture in the Kunu-ri sector, late November 1950. (© Hulton-Deutsch Collection/CORBIS/Corbis via Getty Images)

EUSAK's withdrawal from the Chongch'on, November 28–December 1, 1950

52

the withdrawal. A stubbornly defended Chinese roadblock on the route south from Kunu-ri to Sunch'on caused delays and UNCOM casualties. This roadblock, centered on a pass, was swept with Chinese 38th Army small-arms and mortar fire, and numerous vehicles had been abandoned along the road to block the way south. It was eventually overcome using close air support, employing napalm and strafing fire to wipe out the Chinese troops in the heights above the pass.

EUSAK completed the move to the Sukch'on–Sunch'on–Songch'on line by December 1. The US 2nd Infantry Division had been particularly badly mauled in the Chongch'on fighting and breakout, resulting in 4,940 casualties—around a third of its authorized strength—and the loss of most of its equipment. At the height of the struggle, from November 25 to 30, the division lost 4,446 soldiers. Overall, the division was 8,662 men short. Artillery equipment losses were heavy: out of the division's three artillery battalions, two battalions abandoned or had to destroy all of their weaponry. The artillery battalions lacked 64 howitzers. The 2nd Infantry Division was, for all intents and purposes, combat ineffective. EUSAK had to pull it out of the line on December 1 and move it south of Pyongyang to Yu-li for refit.

Assessing the strategic situation

MacArthur's staff had received multiple reports of intense Chinese activity all along the front. In a JCS message, on November 28, MacArthur stated that UNCOM was now facing "an entirely new war." MacArthur now reversed strategy from the offensive to the defensive. Back in Washington, President Truman and the Pentagon were shocked. Having been ready to prepare for victory, they now feared that MacArthur's command would suffer a calamitous defeat. There was the added issue that the PRC had not declared war, and UNCOM's troops were not officially fighting Chinese forces, complicating the picture considerably on the ground.

Far East Command announced that the anticipated major UNCOM offensive had evolved into a "reconnaissance in force," seeking to assess the nature and scale of the Chinese threat. This announcement fooled nobody: it was clear that MacArthur had been surprised by the PVA's offensive. UNCOM could do little but observe and react to where the PVA would attack next. In Washington, the JCS considered what a massive Chinese intervention meant and its ultimate objectives. At the least, they could expect an increase in fighting tempo with the potential loss of the ROK. At worst, the Chinese attack was a precursor to a larger regional or global war. Perhaps the Soviet Union wanted to enter from the northeast Korean border. Could Moscow use this attack as a pretext for some other action elsewhere in Asia or Europe?

Soon after the PVA had first engaged UNCOM forces, Truman, on November 28, met with his staff to discuss bombing Chinese bases in Manchuria if the situation warranted. Truman still believed that Europe, not Korea, was the key focus for Washington. He had to weigh the impact of escalating the war by using additional B-29 raids on Chinese territory and supporting UNCOM. The JCS had severely limited what MacArthur and his FEAF and Navy carrier forces were authorized to target. In a press conference on November 30, Truman admitted that he had discussed atomic weapons use in Korea, since he evaluated all options to stem the Chinese advance. MacArthur certainly agreed, but UN (especially NATO) members

Chosin Reservoir, November 27–December 11, 1950

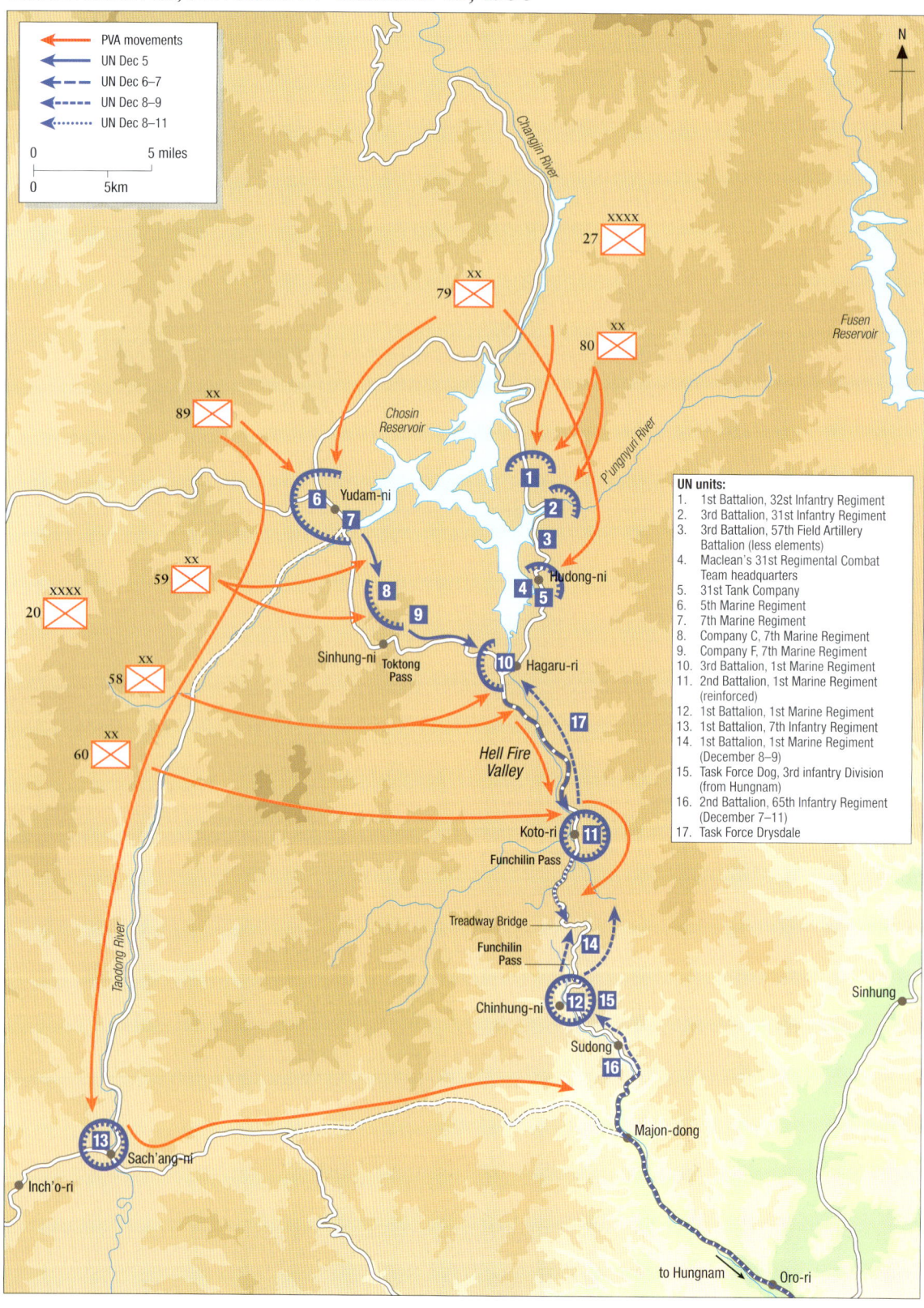

reacted negatively. If Truman used nuclear weapons against China, might the Soviet Union be given carte blanche to do likewise elsewhere?

Still, this encouraged MacArthur to seek approval for atomic bomb release and raised calls by British Prime Minister Clement Attlee for clarification. Attlee's fear was that dropping atomic bombs in Korea would translate to a global war starting in Europe. Truman retreated and the nuclear option evaporated as a serious possibility. Still, others in Tokyo and Washington saw the atomic bombs as a means to signal to Beijing and Moscow the seriousness of the Chinese intervention, to destroy targets not vulnerable to conventional bombing, and believed that leveraging the atomic bomb threat against Beijing and Moscow to halt any further Chinese advances or a move against Western Europe.

With concern about a potential global conflict, MacArthur might not receive additional troops to combat the renewed KPA and fresh PVA units. Generalissimo Chiang Kai-shek, leader of the deposed Nationalist Chinese forces on Taiwan, offered over 33,000 combat soldiers to UNCOM. MacArthur had earlier asked Washington to approve this transfer, but the Truman administration rebuffed the offer so as not to cause additional complications with Beijing. Now that Chinese units were fighting UNCOM, the latter was a moot point. Truman was still concerned about broadening the war and Chiang's entry into the conflict might provoke Beijing into intervene in other areas like Hong Kong, Taiwan, or French Indochina.

The east: Chosin Reservoir, November 27–December 11, 1950

In mid-November, a severe cold snap had struck the north of the Korean peninsula. Falling temperatures, snow, and ice transformed the environment, and made control of the road network even more vital as the ability to move cross-country was limited. The bad weather also affected supply efforts, and would play a major factor in deploying reinforcements or conducting any form of movement.

Two US Marines manning a Browning machine gun prepare to defend against a Chinese attack. The latter often came at night and early in the morning in "human waves." (US Marine Corps)

Troops from the US 1st Marine Division's 7th Infantry Regiment near Yudam-ni in November 1950. (US Marine Corps)

Major-General Oliver P. Smith's 1st US Marine Division was to advance along the Chosin Reservoir's western edge in an effort to meet up with the ROK II Corps, before driving on to the Chinese border at the Yalu River. The planned route required the Marines to pass through steep, rugged terrain where the risk of ambush was ever present. Advancing on the Chosin Reservoir's eastern shore was the US 7th Infantry Division's 31st RCT, under Colonel Allan MacLean. MacLean's 31st RCT had relieved the USMC 5th Infantry Regiment.

MacArthur had recalled Almond and Walker to Tokyo for consultations. After this meeting, considering Walker's situation, Almond directed the 1st Marine Division to move north, then west to sever the PVA's supply lines at Mupyong-ni. With the 7th Infantry Division on his right flank, Smith could sandwich the PVA between his forces and the EUSAK. Concerns were raised by Smith, who had a difficult relationship with Almond: this advance over a very broad front would pit two divisions against several known PVA armies and KPA forces. There would also be a long, vulnerable logistical tail to the coast. Enemy attacks along UNCOM supply lines could easily cut his lines of communications, and there was the risk of encirclement.

The Chinese strategy for countering the move toward and beyond the Chosin Reservoir was centered on eliminating the UNCOM units at Yudam-ni, Sinhung-ni, and Hudong-ni, before advancing on Hagaru-ri. Any relieving UNCOM forces attempting to come to the aid of these units could be enveloped on the road between Hungnam and Hagaru-ri.

Chinese troops engaged the 1st Marine Division and 31st RCT on November 27. Using massed night attacks the PVA's 89th Division (20th Army) and 79th Division (27th Army) drove into the 5th and 7th Marine regiment elements to the west and north of Yudam-ni. Some 89th Division elements also moved south parallel to the road controlled by the US 1st

US Marines watch a F-4U Corsair strike on enemy positions at Hagaru-ri on November 26, 1950. (US Marine Corps)

Marine Division that connected Smith to Hungnam. In an effort to surround the Marines at Yudam-ni, the Chinese 59th Division attempted to divide the two Marine regiments from the headquarters at Hagaru-ri. The 59th Division troops moved towards Sinhung-ni, seeking to capture the Toktong Pass, which controlled the route south to Hagaru-ri. The PVA's 58th Division moved east to attack Hagaru-ri from the south. The 60th Division pushed further south to interdict any UNCOM movements on the road leading north from Koto-ri to Hagaru-ri. The Marine elements north of Hagaru-ri now looked to have been cut off.

East of the Chosin: 31st Regimental Combat Team

On the eastern side of the reservoir, troops from the PVA 80th Division (27th Army) struck MacLean's 31st RCT, whose elements were spread out. Each battalion was out of position to support its neighboring units, and the RCT was vulnerable to defeat in detail by the Chinese.

Almond arrived at the front on November 28 to assess the situation and exhort his subordinates to fight. Contemptuous of the Chinese capability, Almond considered the enemy soldiers were merely stragglers from a retreating force. He dismissively told MacLean's staff: "We're going all the way to the Yalu. Don't let a bunch of Chinese laundrymen stop you."

On November 27, at 2200hrs, the PVA's 80th Division had separated the 31st RCT by isolating the lead 1st Battalion, 32nd Infantry Regiment about four miles north of the 3rd Battalion, 31st Infantry. In between the two battalions, MacLean deployed a mortar company that supported both infantry battalions when the Chinese struck. PVA units also encircled the 3rd Battalion and elements of the 57th Field Artillery Battalion. Since the Chinese had hit the 57th Field Artillery Battalion directly and cut its communications lines, the artillerymen were unable to provide any meaningful indirect fire

CHOSIN RESERVOIR, NOVEMBER 27–29, 1950

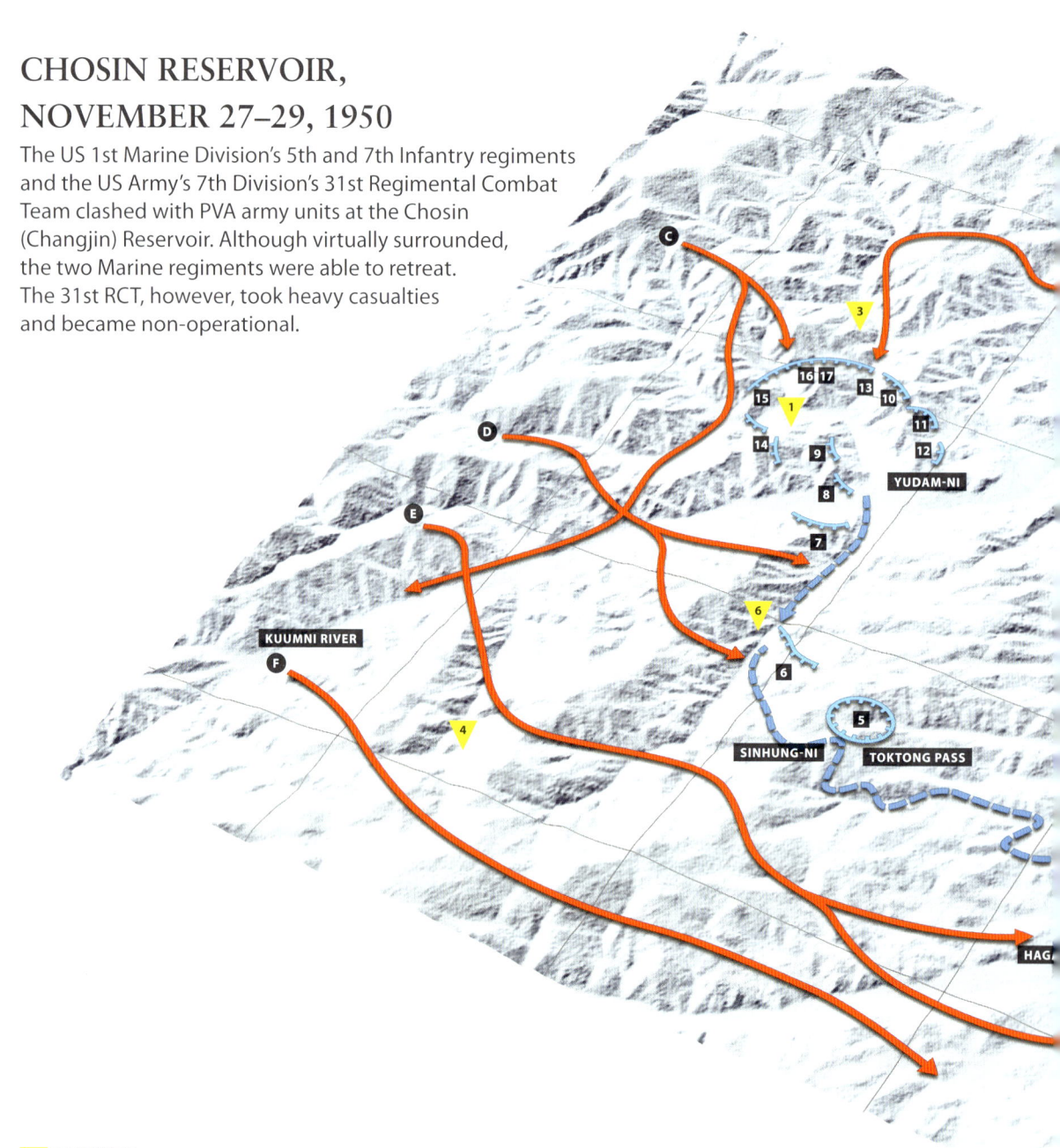

The US 1st Marine Division's 5th and 7th Infantry regiments and the US Army's 7th Division's 31st Regimental Combat Team clashed with PVA army units at the Chosin (Changjin) Reservoir. Although virtually surrounded, the two Marine regiments were able to retreat. The 31st RCT, however, took heavy casualties and became non-operational.

EVENTS

1. Major-General Oliver P. Smith, US 1st Marine Division commander, has deployed his 5th and 7th regiments to prepare to advance to the Yalu River. Smith is concerned about reports from captured Chinese prisoners that indicate several PVA divisions are readying to attack his positions. Although civilians indicate a large Chinese presence, US 1st Marine Division intelligence sources are unable to locate any sizable PVA units. Smith has doubts that the potential US X Corps' offensive can succeed and is concerned about his long supply lines stretching south across narrow passes, which are vulnerable to attack.

2. Major-General David G. Barr, US 7th Infantry Division commander, has sent the 31st RCT (under Colonel Allan MacLean) to protect the US Marine's right flank on the Chosin Reservoir's eastern shore. The RCT is scattered throughout several positions north of Hagaru-ri.

3. During the night of November 27, the PVA 20th and 27th armies begin night attacks against the USMC defensive positions west of Yudman-ni, and against the 31st RCT positions north of Hagaru-ri.

4. The PVA 58th and 60th divisions move against Hagaru-ri from the west, seeking to cut off any means of retreat, supply, and reinforcement for the UNCOM units at the reservoir. The attacks fail to capture Hagaru-ri.

5. The 31st RCT begins to retreat south in the face of Chinese attacks. The PVA 80th Division has isolated the 3rd Battalion, 31st Infantry Regiment using roadblocks. Lieutenant-Colonel Don Faith's 1st Battalion, 32nd Infantry Regiment is subjected to major Chinese attacks. The US X Corps commander Major-General Almond tries to push MacLean to attack and states there are only limited Chinese troops in the area. With Faith's battalion surrounded and running out of ammunition, MacLean orders Faith to move south on November 29.

6. Chinese forces cut the road between Yudam-ni and Hagaru-ri. The US Marine 5th and 7th regiments manage to break out of Yudam-ni and begin moving along the road to Hagaru-ri.

7. MacLean is killed, and Faith takes command of the remaining 31st RCT elements. Units from Hudong-ni, including armor, attempt a link up with it, but fails to do so. Close air support and air-dropped supplies help the RCT. Some troops opt to abandon the road south and head for Hagaru-ri on the frozen Chosin Reservoir.

8. The surviving troops from the US Marines and the 31st RCT reach Hagaru-ri. Smith readies his force to withdraw south to Hungnam in an orderly manner.

Note: gridlines are shown at intervals of 10km (6.2 miles)

PVA
A. 80th Division
B. 79th Division
C. 89th Division
D. 59th Division
E. 58th Division
F. 60th Division

US
1. 1st Battalion, 32nd Infantry Regiment
2. 3rd Battalion, 31st Infantry Regiment
3. 57th Field Artillery Battalion (less elements)
4. 31st Infantry Regiment HQ; 31st Tank Company
5. Company F, 7th Marines (Fox Hill)
6. Company C, 7th Marines (less elements)
7. Company B, 7th Marines
8. Platoon, Company C, 7th Marines
9. Company A, 7th Marines
10. Company E, 7th Marines
11. Company D, 7th Marines
12. 1st Battalion, 5th Marines
13. 3rd Battalion, 5th Marines
14. Company D, 5th Marines
15. Company E, 5th Marines
16. Company F, 5th Marines
17. Company H, 7th Marines

CHOSIN RESERVOIR

P'UNGNYURI RIVER

HUDONG-NI

PAEGAMNI RIVER

NGNAM

SMITH

BARR

59

support to the 1st Battalion, 32nd Infantry. The massed Chinese maneuvers threatened to overwhelm and crush MacLean's battalions, but the soldiers fought on and inflicted significant Chinese casualties. MacLean's lead battalion relied on Marine close air support to stave off the PVA attacks. MacLean's headquarters, at Hudong-ni, tried to reinforce the units under attack with two platoons (14 tanks) from the 31st Tank Company. The tanks, however, found it extremely difficult to move on the ice-packed roads due to the weather conditions, which helped antitank-armed Chinese troops to halt the armor advance. Having lost two tanks that slid off the road, the remaining tanks retreated back to Hudong-ni. MacLean's forces continued to incur casualties, and an intelligence and reconnaissance platoon died to the man as it attempted to move forward.

Any chance of a further UNCOM advance from the Chosin Reservoir was now virtually impossible. The 1st Battalion, 32nd Infantry Regiment was ordered south to join the 3rd Battalion, 31st Infantry Regiment. Early on November 29, MacLean and the 1st Battalion's commander Lieutenant-Colonel Donald Faith withdrew south. The PVA had resumed attacks on the 3rd Battalion, 31st Infantry Regiment and had blocked the path south by occupying a bridge. Faith's men managed to push the Chinese back. As MacLean's HQ moved toward the battalion perimeter, what appeared to be UNCOM reinforcements were spotted approaching; they were actually PVA troops. As they approached to meet them, Colonel MacLean was shot several times and captured; he would die four days later from his wounds.

Faith now assumed command of the forces available, informally renamed Task Force Faith. The 31st RCT had suffered several hundred casualties in two days of intense combat; the 3rd Battalion had barely survived, resulting in 300 casualties. As the UNCOM forces attempted to hold off the Chinese assaults, they were running short of supplies. Faith, aware that the PVA attacks might overwhelm his force at any time, lost contact with the 1st Marine Division and the US 7th Division.

The remnants of the former 31st RCT now began to withdraw south to Hudong-ni. The regimental headquarters, 31st Tank Company, elements of the 57th Field Artillery Battalion, and other support units fell back. Faith was actually unaware of this until the 7th Infantry Division's commanding officer, Major-General David G. Barr, arrived by helicopter to confer with him. Barr ordered a withdrawal from Faith's position to Hagaru-ri at the southern tip of the reservoir. It was now clear to X Corps' leadership that both the US Marines and TF Faith would have to withdraw further south. In trucks loaded with hundreds of wounded, Faith's men would need to negotiate several vulnerable points along the route where the Chinese might inflict heavy casualties, particularly with night attacks when air cover was not available.

TF Faith continued to receive rations and ammunition from Fifth Air Force transports, and USMC Corsair fighter-bombers conducted close air support missions. MacLean had previously requested reinforcements from the south to be sent forward, but it had required time to organize the rail and truck transportation. The reinforcement effort was, however, now gaining momentum, although these units would have to fight through Chinese strongpoints and blocks on the frozen passes leading to the reservoir.

Task Force Faith began to withdraw south on December 1. After destroying all abandoned equipment and supplies, the task force embarked onto the 30

The Chinese attacks, poor weather, the challenging terrain, and the narrow mountain roads shown here, made the US Marines' retreat south from the Chosin Reservoir legendary. (US Marine Corps)

available trucks and moved off shortly after 1200hrs. In the lead was a twin 40mm antiaircraft artillery self-propelled vehicle. Tragically, a USMC close air support aircraft assigned to clear a path for TF Faith unloaded its napalm on the UNCOM truck column in error, inflicting further casualties and causing morale to plummet throughout the column. The column split into isolated packets of vehicles and soldiers moving independently, which came under Chinese small-arms fire. The helpless wounded, and the vehicle drivers, suffered the most as rifle and automatic fire ripped through the trucks. Two miles north of Hudong-ni, the column attempted to cross a bridge near Hill 1221 that had been destroyed by Chinese troops. This delayed the retreat by two hours. Once the trucks had forded the river, they negotiated additional Chinese obstacles and came under fire from Hill 1221. Faith took charge of a mixed contingent of soldiers that stormed the hill, and eventually dislodged the Chinese. However, in the attack, Faith was mortally wounded.

Chinese troops continued to harass the column as it contnued south that evening and into the next day. Some soldiers abandoned their vehicles and retreated over the now frozen Chosin Reservoir in an effort to reach Hagaru-ri safely. Others passed Hill 1221 and headed south to the abandoned Hudong-ni, now dominated by PVA units that were above the town's ridgeline. The 15 remaining trucks in the TF column resumed the journey to Hudong-ni. However, there was insufficient room on the trucks for all of the wounded and some were left behind near Hill 1221 with a protection force, in the hope that an effort might be made to rescue them later. The presence of Chinese soldiers in the town meant that the retreating UNCOM soldiers could not breakthrough and many opted to move across the frozen Chosin. Of the original 2,500 31st RCT soldiers, only 1,000 escaped to Hagaru-ri, with 385 men fit for duty. The US Marines rescued 319 men from the reservoir.

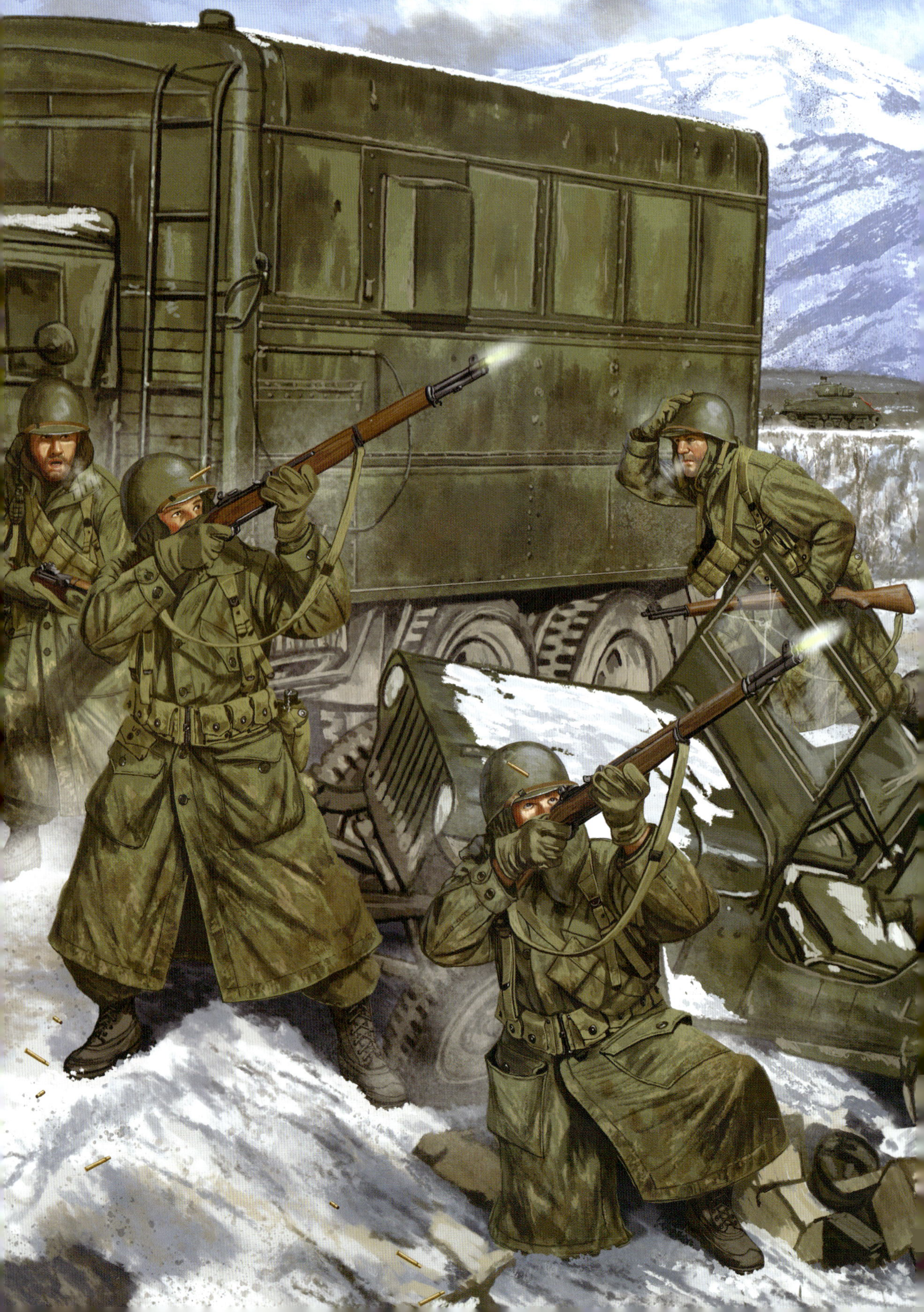

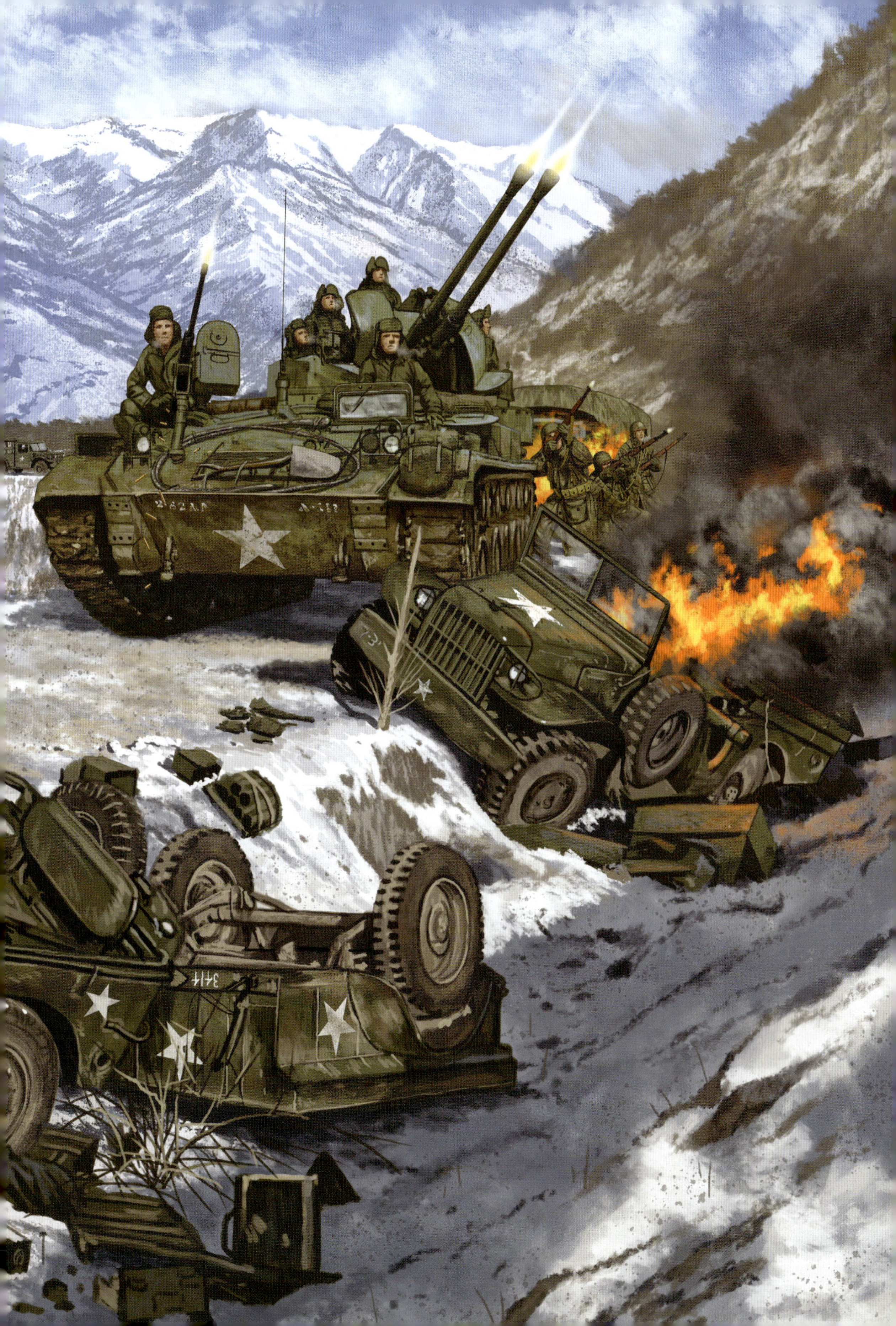

THE RETREAT OF TASK FORCE FAITH, NOVEMBER 27, 1950 (PP. 62–63)

The role assigned to Colonel Allan MacLean's 31st Regimental Combat Team (informally known as Task Force Faith) by Major-General Almond, commander of the US X Corps, was to support the main effort made by the US 1st Marine Division attacking northwest from the Chosin Reservoir. The regiment-sized force was to guard the Marines' eastern flank, occupying the eastern side of the reservoir. However, the nature of the terrain had made it hard to effectively coordinate its operations with the USMC units on the southern and western sides of the Chosin.

By 27 November, the force's units (comprising the 3rd Battalion, 31st Infantry Regiment; 1st Battalion, 32nd Infantry Regiment; two batteries from the 57th Field Artillery Battalion; and a platoon from Battery D, 15th Antiaircraft Battalion) was spaced out in two separate positions stretching 10 miles down the reservoir's eastern side. Here, it was struck by a surprise Chinese attack. Although Almond attempted to convince MacLean to continue the planned offensive operations, the situation on the ground had clearly changed. Lacking the promised reinforcements, the now surrounded Task Force elements found themselves cut off from their lines of retreat to the south by a Chinese roadblock north of Hagaru-ri. US Army units attempted to reach the Task Force, but were forced back.

Chinese attacks on MacLean's force continued during the night of November 28/29. As the weather conditions deteriorated and the temperatures plummeted, mobility became more difficult. Close air support and much-needed supplies were provided by USMC and US Navy planes.

When MacLean was shot and captured by Chinese troops, Lieutenant-Colonel Don Faith took command. The Task Force continued to fight off heavy Chinese attacks, but with ammunition running low and casualties mounting, it was becoming clear that a breakout attempt southward would be necessary. The breakout began on December 1 down the east of the reservoir, with the UNCOM truck column coming under repeated Chinese attack.

Troops from Task Force Faith are shown here returning fire on Chinese troops in the hillsides above them during the breakout. Providing direct fire support is an M19 Multiple Gun Motor Carriage (**1**), armed with two Bofors 40mm guns (**2**), in an M4 mounting. The M19 carried an ammo load of 350 clip-fed rounds, which could be fired at up to 120 rounds per minute; further ammunition was usually towed in an M28 trailer. This M19 is also armed with a Browning .50-cal. machine gun (**3**). The M19's twin 40mm guns' high rate of fire was especially effective against Chinese massed infantry attacks.

Although some survivors of the Task Force would eventually make it through to Hargaru-ri after running the gauntlet of Chinese fire, Faith was not among them: he died from wounds inflicted by a Chinese grenade during the withdrawal.

West of the Chosin: 5th and 7th Marines

Like the 31st RCT, on the western side of Chosin Reservoir Smith's 5th and 7th Marine regiments encountered a brutal Chinese onslaught. The two Marine regiments underwent withering assaults by the PVA's 79th and 89th divisions. The Chinese 59th Division moved round from the south to surround the two regiments. Chinese human wave charges throughout the night convinced Smith that a withdrawal was the only realistic means of avoiding the 5th and 7th regiments' annihilation. Almond agreed and ordered the destruction of all unnecessary equipment and supplies so that they would not fall into Chinese hands. Smith, however, decided to retreat with his equipment intact, and transporting all wounded, on December 1.

The success of the breakout depended on securing the Toktong Pass. The road at the pass was narrow and contained hairpin turns that were difficult to negotiate; moreover, the surface was poor and frequently covered in ice. The surrounding terrain was steep and dominated the road. The Toktong Pass was also now in Chinese hands.

Smith ordered the 3rd Battalion, 7th Marine Regiment to attack south and capture hills 1542 and 1419, which covered the road from Chinese attacks; this allowed the breakout convoy, with a single Sherman in the lead, to pass through 3rd Battalion's positions in the afternoon of December 1. Then, to secure the Toktong Pass, the 1st Battalion, 7th Marine Regiment attacked toward the isolated Company F (Fox), 7th Marine Regiment, which still held the key hill overlooking the vital pass. Fox Company had held out for five days in the face of constant PVA attacks by 59th Division troops. On the morning of December 2, a joint attack by 1st Battalion, 7th Marine Regiment and Fox Company captured the Toktong Pass, opening the road between Yudam-ni and Hagaru-ri for the 5th and 7th Marines to pass through. Marine Fighter Attack Corsairs bombed Chinese positions above the road that continued to harass and impede the column's slow progress south. The breakout convoy finally made it to Hagaru-ri on the afternoon of December 3.

Reviewing the overall situation at this point, MacArthur believed that EUSAK was more vulnerable to destruction than X Corps. He directed Almond to evacuate all of his X Corps through Hungnam and then redeploy units by sea to Pusan, where these forces could reinforce EUSAK. The commanding officer of Fifth Air Force's Combat Cargo Command, Major-General William H. Tunner, offered to fly out Smith's command from Hagaru-ri. Tunner, who had directed the 1948 Berlin Airlift, requested that any vehicles, heavy equipment pieces, and excess supplies be destroyed. Smith rejected the idea since he wished to preserve these assets to reinforce EUSAK.

Marine Tech Sergeant Robert W. Arsenault interrogates Chinese prisoners in the US 7th Marine Regiment positions at the Chosin Reservoir, assisted by a South Korean interpreter. (FPG/Archive Photos/Getty Images)

The US Marine Corps used the M-4 Sherman tank mostly as a close support weapon to aid infantrymen in attack or to repel Chinese mass attacks. Although an older design, the Sherman proved a vital element to the US 1st Marine Division throughout the Korean War. (US Marine Corps)

South from Hagaru-ri: Hell Fire Valley

Hagaru-ri had become a vital supply location, and an airfield was also under construction there. Chinese attacks had begun on November 28, with all UNCOM personnel called to take part in the defense. The Chinese had also blocked the road leading south from Hagaru-ri, and several key bridges had been destroyed. The USMC and US Army personnel managed to hold off the

US Marines hold Chinese prisoners during the retreat south from the Chosin Reservoir. Marine patrols typically paralleled the march of the retreating UNCOM columns and frequently fought Chinese patrols on the steep mountain sides. (US Marine Corps)

This photo illustrates the conditions Smith's US 1st Marine Division faced during the move south to Hungnam. Freezing temperatures and snow restricted movement and slowed the 5th and 7th regiments. The cloud cover also limited close air support missions. The Marines did have armor, like this M-26 Pershing, to act as mobile artillery. (US Marine Corps)

attacks by the PVA 58th Division, with the support of air attacks by VMF-542. The 58th Division would be broken by its efforts to take Hagaru-ri by December 1.

The 3rd Infantry Division had organized a relief column, TF Dog, to drive from Hungnam and escort the UNCOM elements south. TF Dog was to rendezvous with Smith near the Funchilin Pass north of Chinhung-ni, some 30 miles north of Hamhung. The bridge at the pass had been destroyed by the Chinese, and engineers from TF Dog would need to rebuild it. TF Dog contained a battalion from the 7th Infantry, an armored field artillery battalion (self-propelled artillery), engineers, a truck battalion, and other support forces, and was commanded by Brigadier-General Armistead D. Mead. The route between Kot'o-ri to Chinhung-ni would be challenging, with steep inclides and exposure to Chinese fire. To the southwest of Kot'o-ri, a single battalion—1st Battalion, 7th Infantry Regiment (3rd Infantry Division)—protected the left flank on the parallel road running south from Yudamni to Sach'ang-ni, alongside the Taodong River.

A relieving force put together by Colonel Lewis B. "Chesty" Puller, the highly decorated US 1st Marines commander, was assembled at Kot'o-ri, tasked with reaching the UNCOM units at Hagaru-ri. This force comprised the British 41st (Independent) Commando (Royal Marines); B Company, 1st Marines; and ROK personnel. It was named Task Force Drysdale, for its commander British Lieutenant-Colonel Douglas Drysdale.

With a force of some 920 troops, Drysdale moved out in the afternoon of November 29 heading north to Hagaru-ri. Puller had assigned Drysdale four armor platoons to support the drive north. Drysdale's task force came under repeated Chinese attack from 60th Division troops along the road. As it fought its way into Hagaru-ri that evening, PVA gunners destroyed a truck in the middle of the column. The damaged vehicle split the column, blocking the path of troops in the rear, who were then badly mauled by Chinese

For the US 1st Marine Division and the remnants of the 31st RCT, the retreat from the Chosin Reservoir was a tough slog. The Chinese divisions threatened to surround UNCOM forces at almost every turn. The freezing temperatures made survival, let alone combat effectiveness, a difficult challenge every day. (US Marine Corps)

fire. This section of the road was later named "Hell Fire Valley." Some 300 men from the front section of the column reached Hagaru-ri while a further 300 or so managed to make it back to Koto-ri; the remainder were killed, captured, or wounded.

With the USMC troops from Yudam-ni having arrived by December 4, the UNCOM forces at Hagaru-ri could finally begin their breakout toward Hungnam. Their withdrawal south began on December 6, with the 7th Marines at the front and the 5th Marines bringing up the rear.

Despite Chinese attacks headed by recently arrived reinforcements, the Marines manged to hold off the Chinese, and inflicted heavy losses on the enemy. As the column moved south, the high ground dominating the road on either side was secured by UNCOM troops. Kot'o-ri was reached on December 7. Fifth Air Force, US Navy, and US Marine Corps aircraft provided close air support. The battered Chinese 20th Army now attempted to drive east to cut the route south of the UNCOM units. The remnants of the 58th and 60th divisions reached Funchilin Pass, destroyed a key road bridge, and dug in to await the arrival of the column from the north. Many would freeze to death in their foxholes on Hill 1081. Troops from 1st Battalion, 1st Marine Regiment attacked and captured Hill 1081 from the south on December 9.

To repair the destroyed bridge and allow vehicles to continue their movement south, the UNCOM units would require four M-2 Treadway bridging sections. Eight C-119s from Fifth Air Force, each aircraft hauling a 2,500-lb bridge section, parachute-dropped the materials to engineers on the ground. One bridge section was destroyed and another fell into Chinese hands upon landing. The bridge repair was completed on December 9, the engineers assembling the bridge spans under fire. The transit across the Funchilin Pass continued through the night. FEAF allocated all C-119s in

The US X Corps withdrawal from the Chosin Reservoir was slow, with convoys halted by Chinese roadblocks and destroyed bridges. (US Marine Corps)

theater to support X Corp's evacuation, bringing in tons of relief supplies. All the UNCOM units had moved through the pass by December 11. The repaired span was then destroyed to slow the advancing Chinese.

The route south to Hungnam was now open. The remaining elements of the battered Chinese 89th Division made a final attempt to intercept the column at Sudong. 3rd Infantry Division troops held off the 89th's attacks and the route south remained open. All UNCOM units made it to the Hungnam perimeter by 2100hrs on December 11.

The Hungnam evacuation, December 12–24, 1950

The next challenge to face X Corps' leadership was the evacuation from Hungnam. Almond's staff needed to coordinate the evacuation over a shrinking 45-mile defensive perimeter and the loading of men and equipment. The troops to be evacuated included the US 1st Marine Division, the ROK II Corps, and the US Army 3rd and 7th Infantry divisions plus the Hungnam area supply points. The defensive perimeter was gradually shrunk across three evacuation phase lines, as men, equipment, supplies, and any refugees left to avoid the advancing PVA 27th Army (79th, 80th, and 81st divisions) and two KPA division equivalents.

The evacuation started with the US 1st Marine Division sailing out December 12–15. Next, the ROK II Corps embarked between December 15

The US X Corps used captured trains to move men and materiel from the Chosin Reservoir to Hamhung and on to the port of Hungnam. US Engineers destroyed a span of this rail bridge over the Songch'on River, and then pushed a locomotive over the breach. They would later set fire to the wooden repair supports to complete its destruction on December 15, 1950. (US Army)

and 17. The depleted US 7th Infantry Division evacuated the port December 18–21. The US 3rd Infantry Division was the last major unit to leave, completing its withdrawal on December 24.

Aiding the evacuation was the FEAF's Combat Cargo Command that used Yonp'o, an airfield south of Hungnam. US Marine and US Navy aircraft flying out of Yonp'o evacuated the wounded and conducted close air support missions. The airlift operations began soon after 1st Marine Division elements arrived in Hamhung. In two days, starting on December 12, Tunner's crews flew out 340 tons of cargo. From December 14 to 17, Combat Cargo Command went into full operations. Using all available C-119s, C-47s, C-54s, C-46s, and other service aircraft, the aircrews took out 228 wounded, 3,891 military and civilian passengers, and 2,087 tons of cargo to Pusan or Taegu. Expedited turnarounds and a maximum sortie effort allowed Tunner's crews to fly 393 missions.

As the last units departed from the port by sea, the US 3rd Infantry Division's 10th Engineer Battalion and Navy Underwater Demolition teams prepared to destroy any left-behind supplies, ammunition and ordnance, and the Hungnam port facilities. By 1430hrs, the port facilities had been reduced to wreckage.

The US 3rd Infantry Division provided security for the defensive phase lines as UNCOM units and refugees evacuated Hungnam in December 1950 on board US Navy ships. These soldiers from the 3rd Infantry Division's 7th Infantry Regiment are shown preparing local rice to supplement their rations as they hold the perimeter around Hungnam. (US Army)

The US X Corps evacuation from Hungnam was conducted in a disciplined manner. Almond was able to transport ammunition, food, vehicles, and fuel. These supplies would be invaluable as X Corps redeployed to support EUSAK. (US Army)

The pullout from Hungnam was a major success, and has been called one of the greatest evacuations by sea in US military history. Almost 200 ships were involved in withdrawing the UNCOM soldiers, their heavy equipment, and large numbers of refugees. UNCOM forces in the east had suffered major casualties. Combat casuatlies for US X Corps and ROK I Corps amounted to just under 10,500, of which 4,380 were US Marines and 3,150 were US Army. Non-battle casualties caused by the freezing weather added a further 7,000 to the totals.

The air war

Far East Air Forces' mission from early November 1950 was to interdict Chinese troops and supplies flowing into the DPRK, and to destroy the military, industrial, and communications infrastructure of the DPRK. FEAF was not permitted to attack targets within the PRC, and selected electrical generating plants (especially the largest electrical-generating facility on the Sui-ho Dam on the Yalu River) were also off-limits. The DPRK's hydroelectric capacity was very significant. Manchurian industry consumed half of the DPRK's electrical output.

The Chinese expanded their MIG-15 presence near the border, ready to intercept B-29 bombers, whose early escort fighters (such as the F-80 Shooting Star, F-84 Thunderjet, and Grumman F9F Panther) could not match the Soviet fighter's capabilities. This situation forced UNCOM to deploy the only available jet aircraft that could match the MIG-15, the F-86 Sabre.

FEAF commander Stratemeyer's Interdiction Plan No. 4 sought to destroy the rail and road network in the DPRK. Crippling the rail infrastructure would force the PVA to rely on truck transportation to move supplies and personnel. Fifth Air Force intelligence analysts believed the PVA would require 10,000 trucks to maintain its supply system, but it only possessed 4,000 trucks.

An AD-3 Skyraider from TF 77 has just missed hitting a bridge at Sinuiju on the Yalu River. Crews could only strike bridges on the Korean side, and had to dodge antiaircraft artillery and later MIG-15s to hit their targets. The bridge campaign had limited success. (US Navy)

Over 172 infrastucture targets were identified by FEAF, to include railway and highway bridges, tunnels, marshalling yards, and supply centers. There were insufficient B-29-wing and US Navy TF 77 assets to strike all these targets simultaneously. Due to other global demands and priorities, two B-29 wings assigned to the Korean War support returned to conducting SAC's nuclear deterrent missions. Three B-29 bombardment wings were based at Okinawa and Yokota. Maintenance requirements, crew availability, and other factors limited the B-29s to conducting on average 24 sorties per day. Fifth Air Force staff members projected that it would require some 13 B-29 sorties to destroy a bridge, meaning that Interdiction Plan No. 4 would take weeks to accomplish. Moreover, damaged bridges and infrastructure elements were often quickly repaired by Chinese and DPRK labor, requiring further B-29 missions.

The main area of contested airspace for Fifth Air Force was "MIG Alley" in the northwestern DPRK, where the Yalu River empties into the Yellow Sea. In this area, UN fighter pilots battled MIG-15s in an effort to gain air superiority. Once Pyongyan had fallen to UNCOM, F-86 Sabres, under the 4th Fighter Interceptor Wing, were able respond quickly to any MIG-15 presence in MIG Alley. The F-86 was similar in performance to the MIG-15. There were two key differences that gave the UN aircrews a distinct advantage over the communists: the combat experience gained in World War II by the FEAF pilots, and their

Chinese MIG-15s posed a very real threat to UNCOM's air capabilities over the peninsula. The US Air Force had to speed delivery of the F-86 Sabre to better contest the skies over the DPRK. (US Air Force)

Although the MIG-15 was in some respects superior to the F-86, the US Air Force had many veteran fighter pilots that had served in World War II, whose experience proved crucial. This gun camera shot shows a MIG-15 under attack by a US Air Force jet. (US Air Force)

superior training. Throughout the Korean War, the F-86 had a kill/loss ratio of 13:1 against the MIG-15.

The interdiction campaign had mixed results. Although MIG-15s suffered hundreds of losses, they were able to interfere with the UN strategic bombing campaign. In addition, Chinese ground forces moved largely at night, safe from air attack, and reducing truck losses carrying supplies and personnel: FEAF did not have an effective fighter or bomber capability to seek out night-travelling vehicles. FEAF bomber crews frequently observed MIG-15s taking-off from bases north of the Yalu River, but could do little except ready to receive an attack. After the Chinese intervention, UN pilots also started to encounter heavier antiaircraft artillery fire, especially near the Yalu River bridges. The Chinese could build up supplies and troops over the border with immunity from attack. UN fighters could not even cross north into China to finish off an aerial kill.

Moscow had stepped up military aid to China and the DPRK in an effort to improve their capabilities relative to the UN forces. This meant that PVA and DPRK columns became more mechanized and were better protected by antiaircraft artillery. UN bombers and fighter-bombers damaged only 50 percent of the Yalu bridges, and of these, Chinese engineers often quickly repaired the bridges or threw pontoon spans across the river. The freezing temperatures from November onwards also allowed Chinese soldiers to transit frozen rivers by foot or truck, and rail lines were even extended over the ice in places. One area in which UNCOM forces did make their mark was in the provision of close air support and interdiction missions, providing responsive firepower to ground commanders.

EUSAK withdraws from the DPRK, December 1–25, 1950

Despite efforts to conduct an orderly withdrawal, some UNCOM units began to panic, realizing they might be cut off by the Chinese. UNCOM's leadership began to reassess the defensive line at Sukch'on–Sunch'on–Songch'on. Walker recognized that the relatively flat terrain held by EUSAK was not the best ground in which to dig in and defend, especially with his divisions needing replacements and equipment.

UNCOM planned four successive defensive lines that would allow EUSAK to cover the withdrawal from the DPRK and potentially south of the 38th Parallel. Line "Able" was south of Pyongyang from Haeju on the west coast to Sin'gye and to Kumhwa. A more defensible position was Line "Baker," south of the Imjin River and running 135 miles across the 38th Parallel. Line "Charlie" ran south of Seoul along the Han River then onward to Hongch'on and to Wonpo-ri on the east coast. Line "Dog" ran from P'yongt'aek on the west coast, through Wonju and on to Wonpo-ri.

With Pyongyang about to fall to the Chinese and KPA advance, EUSAK planned to withdraw further south to Line Baker. The Imjin River created a notable water obstacle, but the image of a static defensive line was an illusion. EUSAK traded space for time until X Corps' divisions arrived from the east to bolster its forces.

The withdrawal took place in a disciplined manner. EUSAK's quartermasters oversaw the transporting of men, bulk ammunition, equipment, and supplies and materiel out of the port of Chinnamp'o through December 5. American surface ships and the British aircraft carrier HMS *Theseus* protected the maritime withdrawal. After the last ships left,

The retreat and advance of UNCOM and communist forces took a toll on bridges, roads, and other infrastructure. Damage to bridges could both halt an enemy's advance, but also hamper a withdrawal. Here the 55th Engineer Treadway Bridge Company assigned to US I Corps attempts to span the Han River on December 9, 1950 (US Army)

UNCOM forces destroyed the port facilities and tons of abandoned supplies and equipment. Walker's men burned or used demolitions to render 8,000 to 10,000 tons of supplies useless to the PVA and KPA. Fifth Air Force aircraft bombed and strafed 15 M-46 tanks left on flatcars. The last UNCOM forces left Pyongyang on December 5. The next day, PVA and KPA troops re-entered the DPRK capital.

As the battered UNCOM forces headed south toward the Imjin River and their next defensive line, the PVA did not press any major attacks against them. However, UNCOM units faced potential North Korean guerrilla activity in their rear and to the east.

The F-84 was a day fighter that was used mainly as a close air support aircraft after the F-86 assumed the air superiority mission. Even though the F-84 performed well, poor weather conditions frequently grounded it, and other aircraft too. (US Air Force)

UNCOM's retreat, November 26–December 15, 1950

The world media continued to raise questions on how UNCOM, having appeared to be on the verge of victory, was now facing a rout. Responding to critics, MacArthur claimed that he was hampered by national policy to fight the war in such a way that he could not win. MacArthur now argued publically that the Truman administration had shackled his command. As a result, he had suffered through poor strategic guidance and leadership limiting the fighting to Korea only, not blockading China, and avoiding bombing north of the Yalu River; he admitted that the PRC was already at war against the United States. Truman was furious that MacArthur advocated expanding the Korean War into a larger conflict. The president was also incensed that MacArthur did not seek nor did he receive permission to comment on foreign policy to the press. The White House responded with a December 5 "gagging order" that restricted release of public statements by military commanders regarding foreign policy to the press until cleared by the State Department.

The UN now faced three stark options: withdrawing entirely from the Korean peninsula, escalating the war, or negotiating a peace. If Truman withdrew and Korea fell to the communists, then what message would this send to countries in danger of falling under Moscow's or Beijing's influence and for any US-backed guarantees for security? Critics who wanted to free China from the communists might complain that Truman let the opportunity to defeat Mao Zedong escape again. Escalating the war might turn this limited conflict into a global one. An expansion of hitting targets in China could ignite fighting in any number of regional areas with heightened tensions. The only politically acceptable option to the UN was one of stabilizing UNCOM positions and negotiating an armistice with the PRC and DPRK.

Fearing an immediate UNCOM collapse, the US Army Chief of Staff General Joseph Collins visited Korea on December 7 and conferred with MacArthur on Bradley's behalf. Collins' opinion was that MacArthur had adequate capability to fend off the PVA assaults. With the X Corps about to leave Hungnam to reinforce EUSAK, MacArthur could hold the Pusan Perimeter against a determined Chinese offensive. However, this would weaken the UN hand in any negotiations with the Chinese and the North Koreans; holding a position further north definitely boosted the UN's bargaining power.

The UN General Assembly passed a resolution for a ceasefire in Korea on December 14. Beijing rejected the offer since the UN had made the proposal without duly authorized PRC representatives participating in the discussions in New York. At the time, Chiang Kai-shek's government spoke for "China." While the UN debated the ceasefire, Truman and Attlee had initiated their own discussions to end the war. Collins' visit helped dispel questions about expanding the war effort or evacuating the peninsula. President Truman declared a national emergency on December 15 and he immediately increased the defense budget, implemented wage and price controls, and established economic sanctions against the PRC.

MacArthur had made clear to Walker that he was to hold Seoul unless the PVA and PKA threatened encirclement of his forces. On December 23, while traveling ten miles north of Seoul, Walker's jeep was struck by a truck and he was killed. MacArthur requested that Lieutenant-General Matthew Ridgway, the famed 82nd Airborne Division commander, be his replacement. Ridgway, serving on the Army staff as deputy chief of staff for operations and administration, inherited a tremendous challenge, and immediately departed for Korea. MacArthur decided to give Ridgway full control of both EUSAK and X Corps. MacArthur had micro-managed Walker and Almond's leadership in every prior action. Now, Ridgway was allowed to assume sole field command, allowing him to better coordinate and integrate all of the forces in theater under his direction. Controlling the war from Tokyo and splitting the X Corps command from EUSAK had proved to be major challenges for Walker. Immediately on his arrival, Ridgway began a four-day reconnaissance of the Line Baker front conferring with corps and divisional commanders.

THE CHINESE THIRD PHASE OFFENSIVE, DECEMBER 31, 1950–JANUARY 8, 1951

In the Third Phase Offensive, the PVA attacked UNCOM forces along the 38th Parallel. The offensive forced the evacuation of Seoul on January 3, which fell once again to PVA/KPA forces the following day. Although UNCOM forces were forced to retreat some 50 miles, the offensive overextended PVA's lines of communications, and its troops were exhausted.

UNCOM units aligned along Line Baker were as follows. In I Corps' sector in the west, the US 8th Ranger Company (8213th Army Unit) secured Kanghwa Island, the Turkish Brigade guarded the Han River estuary, the US 25th Infantry Division guarded the lower bank of the Imjin River, and the ROK 1st Division guarded the corps' right flank from positions along the Imjin. The British 29th Infantry Brigade formed the I Corps reserve just outside Seoul. The IX Corps guarded the Wonsan–Seoul corridor along the 38th Parallel, with the ROK 6th Division protecting its left flank and the US

EUSAK mechanized assets head south across the 38th Parallel during the withdrawal of UNCOM forces from the DPRK. Mechanization greatly aided UNCOM's capability in moving rapidly and avoiding entrapment by the PVA and KPA. (US Army)

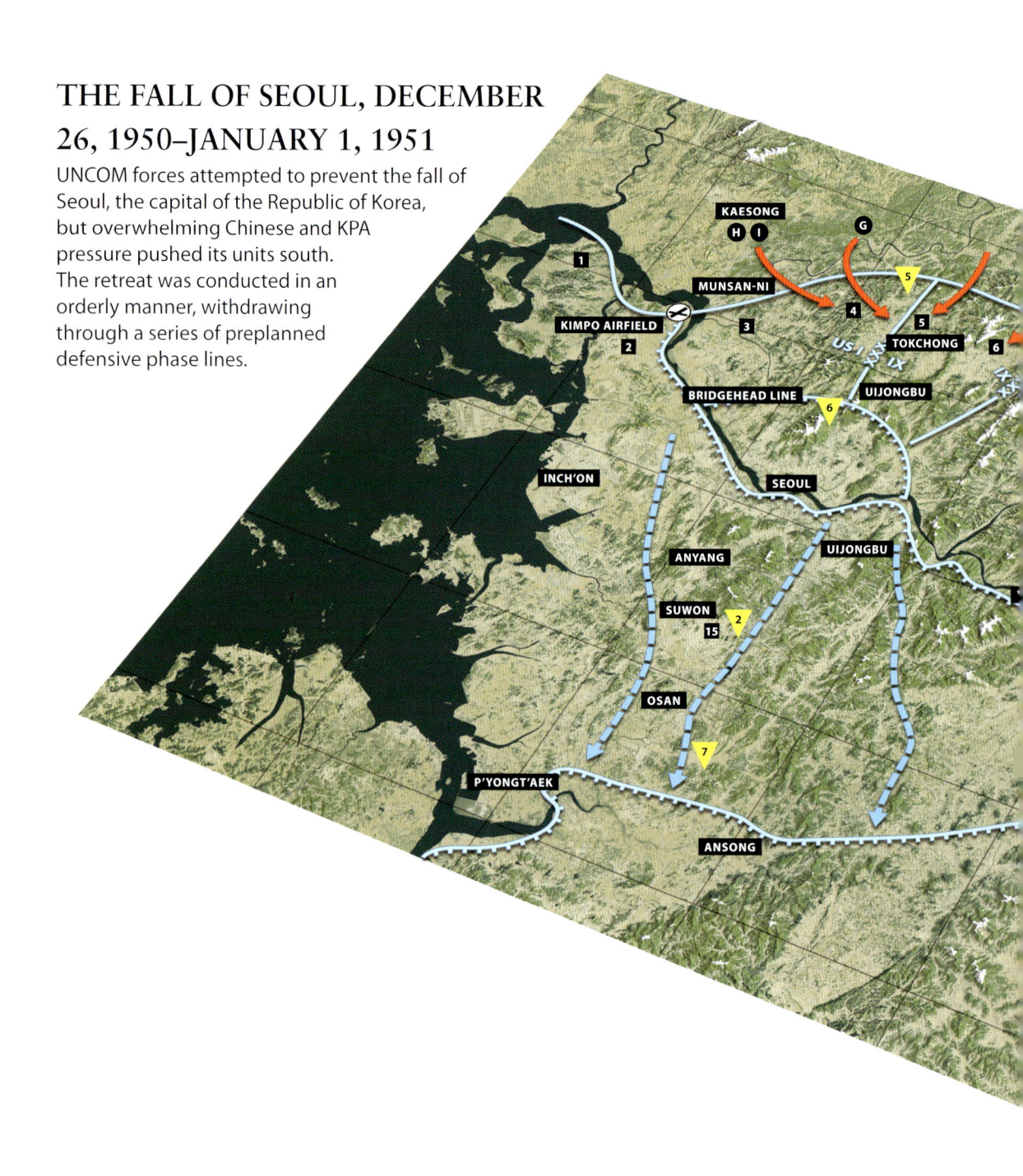

THE FALL OF SEOUL, DECEMBER 26, 1950–JANUARY 1, 1951

UNCOM forces attempted to prevent the fall of Seoul, the capital of the Republic of Korea, but overwhelming Chinese and KPA pressure pushed its units south. The retreat was conducted in an orderly manner, withdrawing through a series of preplanned defensive phase lines.

▼ EVENTS

1. In late November, PVA and KPA units are pushing UNCOM forces rapidly south. To ensure maximum defensive power, the EUSAK staff tries to close as many gaps as possible to contain the Chinese and North Koreans. Seoul looks as if it might be lost once again.

2. The US 187th Airborne RCT at Suwon acts as the reserve force to bolster the EUSAK. Although the paratroopers are mobile, they lack armor and heavy artillery.

3. The PVA and KPA initiate their Third Phase Offensive by picking at UNCOM's weakest link, the eastern defensive areas held by the ROK forces. Moving west, on November 26, the KPA attempts to cut off the EUSAK by pushing toward the west coast.

4. In reaction to a KPA advance, the 5th Regiment, ROK 3rd Division and US 23rd Regiment, 2nd Infantry Division converge on a KPA roadblock south of Hongch'on. The combined ROK and American force stops the North Korean maneuver.

5. On December 31, 1950, and January 1, 1951, the PVA and KPA attack along the UNCOM front line. The communists penetrate gaps between defending regiments and break through.

6. UNCOM units prepare to disengage along their line. Some units concentrate on the planned Bridgehead Line above Seoul, but this will not remain tenable for long.

7. On January 3, 1951, EUSAK units begin to retreat, passing through Line Charlie and on to Line Dog. Seoulis once again in communist hands.

Note: gridlines are shown at intervals of 40km (24.8 miles)

PVA/KPA
- A. KPA II Corps
- B. KPA V Corps
- C. PVA 66th Army
- D. PVA 42nd Army
- E. PVA 40th Army
- F. PVA 38th Army
- G. PVA 39th Army
- H. PVA 50th Army
- I. KPA I Corps

UNCOM
1. US 8th Ranger Company
2. Turkish Brigade
3. US 25th Infantry Division
4. ROK 1st Division
5. ROK 6th Division
6. US 24th Infantry Division
7. ROK 2nd Division
8. ROK 5th Division
9. ROK 8th Division
10. ROK 3rd Division
11. ROK 9th Division
12. ROK Capital Division
13. Regiment (less elements), ROK 23rd Infantry Division
14. 5th Regiment, ROK 3rd Infantry Division
15. US 187th Airborne Regimental Combat Team (reinforced)
16. US 2nd Infantry Division (reinforced)
17. Regiment (reinforced), 23rd Infantry Division

XXXXX PENG DEHUAI

XXXX 8 RIDGWAY

As UNCOM forces withdrew from the DPRK, thousands of civilians followed them south. This put great pressure on ports, roads, and rail lines, and affected the withdrawal of MacArthur's forces. This port scene dated December 19, 1950 shows typical overcrowding. (US Navy)

24th Infantry Division its right. The IX Corps reserve comprised the 27th British Commonwealth Brigade (around Uijongbu) and the US 1st Cavalry Division (the latter included Filipino and Greek units). The ROK III Corps sector saw the ROK 2nd, 5th, and 8th divisions defending the area north of Ch'unch'on, with the ROK 7th Division acting as corps reserve. The ROK II Corps sector lay to its east, with just the ROK 3rd Division blocking access to the Hongch'on River valley. The ROK I Corps protected the EUSAK right flank, with the ROK 9th Division and the ROK Capital Division holding the mountains and the coastal area. X Corps formed Ridgway's front reserve.

Across the front, Ridgway was aware that spirits were generally low. Reinforcements were clearly needed to his units, but time was against him, knowing that a new PVA/KPA offensive was looming. One of his acts as new commander was to raise morale, and gain a much better picture of the enemy strength facing his frontline, through active patrolling and maintaining proper contact with the enemy forces.

The PVA/KPA main forces appeared to be massing in the west center of the peninsula, opposite EUSAK, with an attack most likely to be sent down the roads connecting Wonsan and Seoul. It also appeared likely that the Chinese would also attack through Ch'unch'on in an effort to outflank the US I and IX Corps north of Seoul.

To the northeast of Ch'unch'on, KPA regiments had struck the right flank of the ROK III Corps and at the left of the ROK I Corps. They had reached the rear area of the narrow ROK II Corps sector by December 30 and now were threatening to cut EUSAK's main lines of communication south and east of Seoul. Ridgway moved to reinforce this vulnerable sector with the US 2nd Infantry Division, and sent the 23rd Infantry Division and the ROK 23rd Division to eliminate the KPA incursion, which had now blocked the main road six miles south of Hongch'on. Almond's X Corps would now be brought in to reinfoce the vulnerable Ch'unch'on sector, although it had only recently arrived and its redeployment would take some time to execute. X Corps' initial mission would be to eliminate any PVA/KPA penetrations of the front and protect the IX Corps' eastern flank. The US 1st Marine and 3rd divisions would act as the army reserve, based 40 miles south of Seoul.

The defense of Seoul was also critical. A bridgehead arched from the River Han in the west through Uijongbu and back to the Han east of the city. This line would protect any eventual withdrawal from the ROK capital, shielding the main routes south from enemy artillery fire. The units of US I and IX Corps could withdraw to this line if Line Baker fell.

By 31 December, it was clear the PVA/KPA units were ready to attack south. UNCOM's intelligence identified the KPA I Corps, PVA 50th Army, and PVA 39th Army at the lmjin River; the PVA 38th and 40th armies south of Yonch'on; and the PVA 66th and 42nd armies north of Uijongbu and Ch'unch'on. The KPA II and V corps lay to the east near Hwach'on and Inje, with forces from the PVA IX Army Group expected to move south into this area from Hungnam shortly.

The offensive began on the afternoon of the 31st, with the PVA 116th Division from 39th Army striking forward elements of the ROK 1st Division on the Imjin River and forcing them back. Following a 30-minute artillery barrage, the 116th Division then crossed the lmjin under cover of darkness and attacked the main body of the ROK 1st Division. The attack then broadened to the east, as the PVA 113th Division from 38th Army struck the ROK 6th Division on the left of US IX Corps. At the same time, the PVA 114th Division of 38th Army struck the US 24th Infantry Division on the right of US IX Corps. Shortly afterwards, the PVA 66th Army hit the center of the ROK III Corps sector with an attack against the ROK 5th Division, followed by the ROK 2nd Division on the left of the corps sector. The main

The port of Wonsan was one of the few industrial areas in the DPRK. Here, Fifth Air Force B-26 Invader light bombers drop parachute bombs on supply areas and harbor structures to deny their use to the KPA and PVA. (US Air Force)

effort was clearly targeting Seoul, along the US I and IX Corps boundary, but the eastern attacks by 66th Army were threatening envelopment—a familiar PVA pattern by now.

The ROK divisions, notably the 1st, were being hit the hardest. A night attack by the PVA 116th Division against Paik's ROK 1st Division caused the 12th Regiment to collapse, and by daylight on 1 January some of its subunits had managed to drive into the division's rear, threatening to cut off the adjacent ROK 6th Division under Brigadier-General Chang Do Yong. A V-shaped salient had been driven into UNCOM's frontlines. As Ridgway went forward to assess the situation on the 1st, it became clear to him that although the ROK divisions were attempting to contain the salient, a withdrawal to the Seoul bridgehead line was now advisable: the Chinese were certain to exploit the weakness in the front by sending in reinforcements. Ridgway considered that he had neither the required forces, nor the time to transfer them, to counterattack the salient at this point.

At noon on January 1, 1951, Ridgway ordered the US I and IX corps to pull their units back to the Seoul Bridgehead Line, and for all the ROK forces in the east to withdraw to defensive Line Charlie, stretching from the Han River east to the coastal city of Wonpo-ri. The withdrawal was to take place in daylight, so that it could be protected by UNCOM air cover. The withdrawal would necessitate the evacuation of the major port of Inch'on.

Milburn's I Corps began its withdrawal in contact on the afternoon of the 1st, holding the ROK 1st Division in a forward position until daylight on January 2. It too then withdrew to the Bridgehead Line. All I Corps units relocated without major loss. Coulter's IX Corps units moved south in two stages from Line Baker, beginning on the afternoon of the 1st. As Chinese forces occupied Tokch'on, one regiment from ROK 6th Division was struck hard by PVA 118th Division troops attacking out of the ROK 1st Division sector. The ROK 6th Division's withdrawal began to lose unit cohesion, and over half its troops were lost. Gay's US 1st Cavalry Division moved to cover the gap left in the front by the disorder of the ROK 6th.

The fall of Seoul

By January 2, the UNCOM units had settled at the Bridgehead Line and Line Charlie. With renewed Chinese and KPA attacks imminent, it was clear to all that any UNCOM hold on the Bridgehead Line was unikely to be a long-term tenure. The fact that the Han River had now solidified over increased the vulnerability of Ridgway's forces here, with attacks now possible from PVA/KPA troops crossing its frozen surface. The large numbers of civilians fleeing Seoul complicated matters, cluttering the road network. Ridgway ordered reinforcements into the Bridgehead Line, including a Thai battalion and US 92nd and 96th Field Artillery battalions.

The situation to the west was difficult to assess, as the ROK units appeared to be in a disorganized state and little information was reaching Ridgway's HQ. For this reason, he ordered Almond's US X Corps to assume responsibility on January 3 for a 35-mile sector of Line Charlie, protecting against any PVA/KPA attacks from Ch'unch'on and from the east/northeast. Gaps were appearing also in the ROK I Corps sector in the far east.

The PVA's move to capture Seoul began with an attack from the northwest down the main Route 1 road, striking the UNCOM Bridgehead Line. On the I Corps left, the PVA 50th Army came into contact with the US 25th Infantry

Soldiers from the US 2nd Infantry Division's 19th Infantry Regiment on the move on January 3, 1951. The challenging nature of the terrain is evident. (US Army)

Division in the early hours of January 3. The PVA 39th Army hit the British 29th Infantry Brigade a few hours later, with the brigade being forced from its positions, only to retake them in a counterattack that pushed the Chinese back. At the same time, in IX Corps' sector the 24th Infantry Division was put under pressure by the lead elements of the PVA 38th and 40th armies; again it initially lost ground only to recover it later.

On January 3, 1951, for a second time, UNCOM had to abandon the ROK capital of Seoul to the communists. US Army engineers built pontoon bridges across the Han River to speed the EUSAK's retreat to safety. This Sherman tank was one of last to leave the city; the only remaining bridge over the Han was destroyed on January 4. (US Army)

The bigger picture, however, was becoming clear. Combined with concerns about the KPA II and V corps to the east aiming at Wonju, Ridgway opted to abandon the Bridgehead Line and being the retreat south of the ROK capital Seoul before the situation became unmanageable for UNCOM. The move was no simple operation: over 70,000 UNCOM troops would need to filter over the damaged Han River crossings on their way south, and the moving of key elements of the civilian infrastructure, and civilians themselves, was a complicating factor. Soon the few bridges available might come under Chinese artillery fire or might even be swamped with fleeing civilians.

At midday on January 3, Ridgway ordered the Bridgehead Line units to withdraw to Line Charlie south of the Han River, to be followed by a further withdrawal of EUSAK to Line Dog. Milburn was assigned the role of controlling all traffic crossing the Han River. US I corps units would protect the clearance from Seoul airport, Kimpo airfield, and Inch'on. Ridgway ordered that all usable equipment be withdrawn, as well as any sick, wounded, and dead UNCOM troops. Milburn ordered the 27th British Commonwealth Brigade, as the last unit to leave Seoul, to oversee the destruction of the bridges behind them. The final civilians left the city and crossed the Han River on January 4, when the remaining bridges were destroyed. Most of Seoul's population had by now fled south or into the countryside around the city. The withdrawal was conducted without any major engagement by the PVA or KPA. The DPRK flag was soon seen flying over Seoul City Hall.

The loss of Seoul for a second time was a bitter disappointment. Some on MacArthur's staff viewed the ROK capital's fall as a precursor to another retreat to Pusan, just as UNCOM had to do earlier. However, this time the retreat might present an even greater risk of a communist takeover of the entire peninsula given that China was now in the war.

During the UNCOM retreat from Seoul, US Army engineers dismantled sections of this pontoon bridge on the Han River and then destroyed it on January 4, 1951. (US Army)

AFTERMATH

UNCOM'S COUNTEROFFENSIVE, JANUARY–APRIL 1951

After the fall of Seoul, Chinese attacks in the west of the peninsula weakened. The PVA's focus had now moved eastward, seeking to infiltrate behind the US I and IX corps to capture Wonju and bisect the main UNCOM lines of supply and communication between Pusan and Hongch'on. UNCOM forces pulled back from Wonju on January 7, 1950, and within a few days large numbers of PVA and KPA troops had moved into sector held by the ROK III Corps.

On January 15, 1951, Ridgway planned and then executed Operation *Wolfhound*, another "reconnaissance in force" in the I Corps sector to seek out and destroy suspected Chinese units in northwestern ROK territory. Ridgway's force of 6,000 men led by the US 27th Infantry Regiment pushed north toward Osan and Suwon, meeting little opposition, before returning south.

Pressure on UNCOM units in the central and eastern sectors was gradually easing by the third week of January, although intelligence and reconnaissance indicated that the Chinese and North Korean were stockpuling supplies and bringing in reinforcements.

Ridgway next ordered a UNCOM counteroffensive, which ran from January 25 to April 21, 1951. Elements of the US 1st Cavalry Division conducted a reconnaissance in force commencing January 22, which revealed that PVA and KPA units had withdrawn from their frontline positions. This was followed by a much larger, US–ROK reconnaissance in force codenamed Operation *Thunderbolt* commencing January 25. Like the previous effort, it encountered only light enemy resistance, and was supported by UNCOM air assets. PVA and KPA resistance gradually stiffened through to the end of the month but in early February it began to collapse, and UNCOM forces

A soldier from the US 24th Infantry Division's 19th Infantry Regiment takes a rest at Yoju, southeast of Seoul, on January 10, 1951. Although demoralized, the division maintained cohesion and fought well. (US Army)

After the retreat from Seoul, UNCOM troops from the US 1st Marine Division collect PVA prisoners for processing in early 1951. (National Archives)

had pushed through to Inch'on and to the southern banks of the Han River.

In the center of the peninsula, both Wonju and Hoengsong were taken by UNCOM unist in early February against light resistance. Operation *Roundup* was launched on February 5; this saw the US X Corps striking North Korean forces assembling south of Hongch'on. Greater enemy resistance was encountered in this sector, and on the night of February 11/12, PVA forces

A disabled M4 Sherman from the 32nd Infantry Regiment, 7th Infantry Division waits for infantrymen to clear a patch of ground of mines in February 1951. (US Army)

struck X Corps north of Hoengsong pushing its troops back. Hoengsong was abandoned on February 13, and Chip'yong-ni also fell to PVA/KPA units, despite the efforts of the US 23rd Infantry Regiment and a French battalion to hold off the enemy advance. Elements of the US 7th Division and ROK units had meanwhile held off a strong PVA attack northeast of Wonju.

In the west of the peninsula, further ground was taken by the US I and IX corps as they pushed up to the Han River. A pocket of PVA/KPA troops still held an area between Seoul and Yangp'yong, however, and on the night of February 13/14 they launched a failed attack toward Suwon, suffering heavy losses.

By February 18, it was becoming clear through reconnaissance that the PVA and KPA units in the central sector were pulling back from the front, which led Ridgway to order US IX Corps to push forward. On February 21, Operation *Killer* was launched, led by the US IX and X corps. However, the general advance by both corps became bogged down in the muddy roads caused by the spring melt and heavy rainfall. By February 28, UNCOM had pushed all PVA and KPA units from their positions south of the Han River.

Ridgway's next move was to continue the drive northward in the center and east of the peninsula to secure Line Idaho just south of the 38th Parallel. The operation was codenamed *Ripper*, and was launched on March 7, 1951. Seoul was once again taken by UNCOM forces, without a fight, on the night of March 14/15. By March 17, Line Idaho had been reached.

UNCOM was now fighting for location and territory to influence the war's ceasefire and no longer sought grander objectives like the DPRK's destruction or crushing the KPA. Truman's foreign policy, at least for Korea, concentrated on an armistice. American commanders made limited advances, nothing like MacArthur's actions above the 38th Parallel or the amphibious landings at Inch'on. However, it would not be until July 27, 1953 that UN, Korean, and Chinese negotiators would finally sign a ceasefire, at Panmunjom. For Washington, the overall cost of the war would be 33,651 killed-in-action, 3,262 non-combat deaths, and 4,729 missing while suffering 211,454 wounded. South Korean losses would top 227,800 killed, 717,100 wounded, and 43,500 missing. The PVA and KPA casualties are unknown, but they may have been as high as 1.5 million killed, missing, and wounded. Civilian losses and casualties would stand at around 2 million.

The legacy of the Yalu campaign

After the Yalu campaign, MacArthur's image of the victorious commander who stemmed the communist tide faded. MacArthur blamed subordinates and increasingly Washington for his failure in the field. Truman's Korean political settlement was a concept alien to MacArthur who judged that the only viable option to settle the war was the enemy's total military defeat. This disagreement exploded in 1951. Truman was preparing to announce a new peace proposal to Beijing. MacArthur upstaged this on March 24 by releasing a press statement where he advocated attacking PRC coastal and interior areas. MacArthur enflamed Truman with this open break in foreign policy with Washington. In addition, MacArthur had replied to Speaker of the House of Representatives Joseph Martin's request for comments about a proposed Lincoln Day speech. Instead, Martin read MacArthur's response on the House's floor. In his commentary, MacArthur argued for the UN to employ Nationalist Chinese soldiers to invade the PRC and that America was

South Korea and the United States used a number of devices to weaken KPA soldiers' morale. This leaflet suggests that Josef Stalin, Mao Zedong, and Kim Il-Sung are responsible for continuing the war instead of negotiating a settlement. (US Air Force)

close to fighting World War III. In addition, MacArthur felt "in war, indeed, there is no substitute for victory" on the battlefield vice a negotiated peace. The comments refuted Truman's policy. UN partners, especially the British, were angry and called for MacArthur's immediate removal as UNCOM commander. This was the last straw for Truman. For violating the December gag order and insubordination, Truman dismissed MacArthur and ordered him home on April 11. MacArthur later staged a bid for the Republican nomination for president. This effort failed and his onetime military aide in the Philippines, Dwight Eisenhower, would take the nomination and eventually win the race for the White House over Truman in 1952.

Truman's critics reacted vehemently to MacArthur's relief. The firing proved extremely unpopular among the American public, press, and in Congress. Truman's approval rating dropped to a historic low. However, many in Western Europe cheered the move. The PRC was also glad to see MacArthur dismissed. In the Philippines, Japan, and South Korea, MacArthur's sacking was met with shock and disapproval. Arguably, the most famous and controversial of American World War II commanders, MacArthur had been considered by many as the savior of Asia and the Pacific. Truman did not dodge criticism for MacArthur's firing. Some vocal opponents claimed Truman dismissed MacArthur to deflect attention away from himself for losing the war.

Ridgway successfully rebuilt and led the EUSAK. Upon taking command, he restored order, discipline, and morale—all lacking after the Chinese intervention and subsequent UNCOM withdrawal below the 38th Parallel. After MacArthur's dismissal, Ridgway replaced him as the UNCOM and FEC commander. Ridgway directed that his forces ready themselves for offensive actions, but these engagements only succeeded in restricted terms. He did blunt all the major PVA–KPA offensives launched against UNCOM and instituted several small, key offensive operations to push the PVA–KPA north.

MacArthur began the Yalu campaign with several bold, innovative moves. With the KPA on the run in early October 1950, total victory seemed highly likely and a possible permanent Korean solution appeared at hand. Changing strategy from protecting South Korea's existence and pushing the North Koreans above the 38th Parallel to destruction of the DPRK's military proved fatal. Compounding this error was faulty intelligence. Top intelligence and diplomatic analysts should have voiced more strident concerns regarding the advance of UNCOM forces, particularly American units, to the PRC's border at the Yalu River and Beijing's likely reaction. Underestimating Chinese military capabilities also contributed to the shock and surprise that resulted in sizable UNCOM losses.

For many military commanders in 1950, fighting a limited war was a difficult concept to comprehend. All senior American military leaders were veterans of the total war concept demonstrated in World War II. Still, using war to attain political objectives was not new. Carl von Clausewitz had observed that war was merely a continuation of politics and that war may remain limited in scope depending on political leaders' and their belligerents' stakes in war. MacArthur could not adjust to the situation. True, Clausewitz did believe that complete enemy military defeat may help attain political objectives, but this might not be the ultimate objective. During the Korean War the specter of expanding a limited war to a global one, gaining support from UN countries, and following the policies from Truman as his civilian superior, seem to have been lost on MacArthur. Similarly, Truman remained mildly disengaged with Korea after MacArthur's successful Inch'on landing and his initial offensive that captured Pyongyang. He may have pinned too many hopes, without weighing the risks, of an impending military victory against the DPRK. Further, he hoped a military victory and the DPRK's destruction as a state translated to a needed example of a victory over communism. Only after China entered the fray did Truman realize that the conflict's nature had changed and that MacArthur was correct in stating Washington faced a completely new war.

Still, the war's nature had evolved before the Chinese had entered the struggle. The most critical change in strategic objectives occurred when the UN amended its objectives to repel the DPRK's invasion in June 1950 and only restore the pre-war borders. MacArthur had confided to Collins, on July 13, 1950, that his personal objectives included the KPA's complete destruction and a possible occupation of the DPRK. His military objectives were certainly stronger than the original UN mandate and Collins did not suggest to MacArthur that he should adjust his strategic vision. After Inch'on, neither Truman nor Marshall raised many concerns, other than the obvious caveats about avoiding major conflict with any Chinese or Soviet intervention, regarding MacArthur's authorization to drive above the 38th Parallel and later to the Yalu River. The major decision-makers in Washington

US Air Force Douglas B-26 Invader bombers of the 3rd Bomb Wing (Light) deliver napalm bombs on KPA storage area and barracks in Chongsoktu-ri in the DPRK, February 1951. A B-26 can be seen at upper left starting its bomb run. (US Air Force)

The fighting would continue for two more years. In 1953, representatives from the United Nations and the DPRK signed a ceasefire that did not end the war. The armistice redrew the border and the sides released their prisoners of war, but technically the war continues to this day. (US Navy)

and Tokyo possessed divergent political and military objectives that would plague UNCOM at this stage.

Similarly, the Chinese later repeated problems that the North Koreans suffered at the war's outset. Kim Il-Sung's KPA did achieve strategic surprise when his columns pushed aside the ROK Army and initial American forces sent to slow Pyongyang's advance. The North Koreans started to suffer from extended logistical lines, high numbers of casualties, and irreplaceable equipment losses. The PVA would soon suffer a similar fate following their initial intervention. Ridgway could now call upon his fully mobilized UNCOM forces. In addition, Fifth Air Force, TF-77, and other air assets could provide valuable strike capabilities and transport supplies. The Chinese advances would soon grind to a halt as the UNCOM forces conduct a determined defense in tough terrain.

China's entry into the Korean War also had future implications for another Asian conflict: the Vietnam War. Several key Department of Defense leaders had advocated a conventional invasion of North Vietnam instead of waging a counterinsurgency in the south. Citing concerns over a possible Chinese entry into North Vietnam, the Johnson administration declined to send ground forces against Hanoi above the South Vietnamese border. Without this constraint, Washington may have fought a much different conflict.

One can speculate how the Korean situation might have changed had MacArthur advanced no farther north than a line from Pyongyang to Wonsan. The DPRK would have forfeited major population centers and would only have controlled mountainous terrain not conducive to industrial development or agriculture.

Eisenhower concluded the Korean War's ceasefire. Ironically, Eisenhower, frustrated by stalled negotiations, considered using nuclear weapons against the DPRK and the PRC to end the conflict in January 1953. Secretary of State John Foster Dulles discussed the option of expanding the war if negotiations failed with Indian Prime Minister Jawaharlal Nehru. India, at the time, had relatively good relations with the PRC. Dulles assumed that the Indian Government would transmit the message to Beijing. After the armistice, Eisenhower agreed to use atomic bombs against the PRC if the war erupted again, rather than enduring another limited ground war in Korea.

THE BATTLEFIELD TODAY

The border that lies within buffer zone between North Korea and South Korea (known as the Korean Demilitarized Zone) remains unchanged since the 1953 armistice. This armistice brought about a ceasefire and prisoner repatriation, but not the end of conflict. (A final peace settlement has yet to be achieved; the ROK never signed the Armistice agreement, refusing to accept the division of Korea.) Although the Cold War ended for Europe with the fall of the Berlin Wall in 1989, a division still exists on the Korean Peninsula. The PRC is not in an active military conflict with United States or the UN, in contrast with the DPRK. Tensions continue to arise occasionally provoked by the DPRK's missile testing, artillery fire, border disputes, covert raids, nuclear weapons development, assassinations, and other incidents. These have drawn in regional powers to include Japan and other nations, which may become embroiled in any future dispute, but this time with possible nuclear-armed ballistic missiles.

Several areas fought over during the Yalu campaign are not widely accessible to most individuals. The DPRK, in general, is difficult to enter,

While evacuation from Hungnam, the US 1st Marine Division established a military cemetery and the Marines rendered honors to their fallen comrades at Chosin Reservoir. (US Marine Corps)

as is traveling freely throughout the country. Major transportation means, public and private, within the DPRK are limited, especially for foreign tourists. Before planning a DPRK visit, the traveler must make pre-planned arrangements to include using DPRK tour guides approved by the DPRK's Ministry of Tourism. These travel guides come from government-sanctioned travel services in Pyongyang. Visiting areas such as the Chosin Reservoir or Wonsan may require advance requests and the tour services will need to arrange appropriate transportation. Rental cars are not readily available. Typically, American citizens face stringent restrictions on visiting the DPRK, unless for humanitarian reasons, as part of the news media, or on official government business. Air travel is the predominant entry method into the DPRK. The two main airlines flying to Pyongyang are Air Koryo (the DPRK's national airline) and Air China. Flights to Pyongyang normally originate from Beijing.

Pyongyang has been completely rebuilt since the 1950 fighting. Much of the city's reconstruction was politically driven, using building facades to provide the image of a vibrant capital. Outside the capital, a general lack of infrastructure development and strict internal security has led to controlled access to certain sites, especially military ones. In Pyongyang, one can visit the Victorious Fatherland Liberation War Museum. The museum includes displays featuring captured period vehicles and aircraft. Tour guides present the DPRK's version of the war. They also present alleged American and UN atrocities. In addition, the USS *Pueblo*, a US Navy intelligence-gathering ship seized by the DPRK on January 23, 1968 along with 83 crew, is moored on site along the Potong River. Pueblo is the only US Navy ship still on the commissioned roster currently held captive.

One might be able to visit the DPRK border at the Yalu River from the PRC side. However, train, bus, or pedestrian travel from the border into the DPRK is strictly controlled for those who are not citizens of the PRC or the DPRK. Similarly, entering and exiting the DPRK through the Demilitarized Zone is prohibited unless Pyongyang grants special permission to do so.

Air strikes, artillery barrages, and street fighting inflicted destruction on Seoul during the war. Since then, economic development has spurred construction throughout South Korea. Seoul ranks among the world's top modern cities, in contrast with Pyongyang. The advanced ROK economy has provided the means and needs to develop extensive infrastructure, to include roads and railways, aiding any visitor who wishes to visit areas where the conflict was fought.

In Seoul, one can visit the Korean War Memorial Museum. The museum honors the victims of all the wars fought throughout the Korean Peninsula, to include the 1950–53 conflict. Visitors can see armored fighting vehicles, aircraft, and many period artifacts and displays.

Seoul, the largest city in the ROK and its capital, is home to the War Memorial of Korea. This museum and monument provides an excellent exhibit on the Korean War and wars involving Korea. Entry is free and easy to reach from downtown Seoul. The grounds host several aircraft and combat vehicles relating to the Korean War. (Department of Defense)

The DPRK–ROK border still provokes tensions reminiscent of the Cold War between the Warsaw Pact and NATO. The Korean Demilitarized Zone's "hot spot" is Panmunjom. UN and DPRK representatives continue to discuss a number of issues at the border in these conference rooms, while ROK and US military personnel, and their KPA counterparts, maintain watch on each other. (Department of Defense)

Individuals may arrange tours from South Korea to Panmunjom's Joint Security Area at the Demilitarized Zone. The 2.5-mile-wide, 160-mile-long Demilitarized Zone is still considered an extremely dangerous area. KPA infiltrators have occasionally planted mines in the area and shootings have occurred in the past. North Korean, South Korean, and US guards man border stations and patrol the zone. DPRK engineers have also dug extensive tunnels beneath the border for potential use by infiltrators for a future invasion or clandestine intelligence operation. The Norh Korean 'model' village of Kijŏng-dong is one of two villages permitted to remain in the DMZ; the other is the South Korean village of Daeseong-dong, which lies 2.22km away. The two villages feature some of the tallest flagpoles in the world. Limited visitor access is possible.

If one cannot travel to the Korea, then US residents can enjoy several museums containing Korean War exhibits. This includes the Korean War National Museum at Springfield, Illinois. With limited displays, this museum provides an overview of the Korean conflict. The National Museum of the Marine Corps (located on Marine Corps Base Quantico, Virginia) is a huge facility that traces the service's Korean War actions. The many displays include a Marine Corps perspective on various engagements, to include the Chosin Reservoir. The National Museum of the US Air Force at Wright-Patterson Air Force Base, Ohio provides the visitor the opportunity to examine the main aircraft types used throughout the Korean War. From a B-29 to the iconic F-86 and MIG-15, the museum displays restored aircraft and narrates the USAF's role in the war. The National Museum of the US Navy, Washington Navy Yard, Southeast Washington DC, includes exhibitions including amphibious operations, naval aviation, and other activities. The future National Museum of the US Army will open at Fort Belvoir, Virginia. This museum will include artifacts and activities presenting the Army's combat encounters in the Korean War along with other conflicts.

BIBLIOGRAPHY

Appleman, Roy E., *South to the Naktong, North to the Yalu*, Washington: Center of Military History, 1992

Central Intelligence Agency, *Critical Situations in the Far East*, Washington: Central Intelligence Agency: various reports from 1950 through 1951

Chen, Jian, *China's Road to the Korean War*, New York: Columbia University Press, 1994

Clayton, James D., *Refighting the Last War: Command and Crisis in Korea 1950–1953*, New York: The Free Press, 1993

Cohen, Eliot A., *Only Half the Battle: The Chinese Intervention in Korea, 1950*, Washington: Central Intelligence Agency (n.d.)

Futrell, Robert F., *The United States Air Force in Korea*, Washington: Office of Air Force History, 1983

Headquarters, Eighth United States Army Korea, *Enemy Tactics*, Tokyo: Eighth United States Army, 1951

Headquarters, Far East Command, *History of the North Korean Army*, Tokyo: Far East Command, 1952

Headquarters, United States Army Forces, Far East and Eighth United States Army, *Report on the Psychological Warfare Conducted by the Eight Army Units in Korea 25 June 1950 thru 27 July 1953*, Tokyo: Headquarters, United States Army Forces, Far East and Eighth United States Army, 1954

Headquarters, X Corps, *Special Report on Chosin Reservoir 27 November to 10 December 1950* (n.d.)

Headquarters, X Corps, *War Diary Summaries 1–31 October 1950 Wonsan-Iwon* (n.d.)

Kuhns, Woodrow J. (ed.), *Assessing the Soviet Threat: The Early Cold War Years*, Washington: Center for the Study of Intelligence, Central Intelligence Agency, 1997

Marshall, S.L.A., *Commentary on Infantry Operations and Weapons Usage in Korea Winter 1950–51*, Chevy Chase: Operations Research Office, The Johns Hopkins University, 1951

Mossman, Billy C., *Ebb and Flow November: 1950–July 1951*, Washington: Center of Military History, 2000

Rottman, Gordon L., *Korean War Order of Battle: United States, United Nations, and Communist Ground, Naval, and Air Forces, 1950–1953*, Westport: Praeger Press, 2002

Wainstock, Dennis D., *Truman, MacArthur, and the Korean War*, Westport and London: Greenwood Press, 1999

Whiting, Allan S., *China Crosses the Yalu: The Decision to Enter the Korean War*: Palo Alto: Stanford University Press, 1960